PRINCESS ANNE COUNTY VIRGINIA

LAND AND PROBATE RECORDS

ABSTRACTED FROM

DEED BOOKS ONE TO SEVEN

1691–1755

Anne E. Maling

HERITAGE BOOKS
2013

HERITAGE BOOKS

AN IMPRINT OF HERITAGE BOOKS, INC.

Books, CDs, and more—Worldwide

For our listing of thousands of titles see our website
at
www.HeritageBooks.com

Published 2013 by
HERITAGE BOOKS, INC.
Publishing Division
100 Railroad Ave. #104
Westminster, Maryland 21157

International Standard Book Numbers
Paperbound: 978-1-55613-620-7
Clothbound: 978-0-7884-6969-5

TABLE OF CONTENTS

INTRODUCTION

Princess Anne County, Va. was formed from part of Lower Norfolk County in 1691. With this in mind the researcher will find the very earliest records for this area in Norfolk County. It was not until after the Revolution that deeds and wills were recorded in separate books. Everyone did not leave a will, and sometimes all heirs were not named in a will. Considerable genealogical material may be found in deeds.

This text attempts to abstract family records from 1691 to 1755 for the benefit of the researcher to whom the original records are not readily available. Where names were not legible I have used a ___. After the page notation the first date given is the date a will was written. The second date is the date of probate. The varied spelling of surnames has been retained as a guide to the researcher to look for the name of one's ancestor spelled in more than one way.

In 1962 Princess Anne County was incorporated into the city of Virginia Beach, Va. by which name it is now known. This attempt to present in abbreviated form some of the early records of the area has been made with the gracious permission of J. Curtis Fruit, Clerk of the Circuit Court of the City of Virginia Beach.

DEED BOOK ONE

1DB2   18 Nov 1691:   Peter CRASHLY and Sarah
his wife, only true and lawful heir to Thomas ALLEN
to William HILLYARD for 5000 lbx. of pork a planta-
tion of 250 acres. Wit: William ARTHUR, James PETERS,
Thomas HALL.
    1DB5   8 Jul 1691:   Randolph LOVETT to Thomas
ILISSE 260 acres, part of land given to my brother
John LOVETT, dec. by the last will of my father
Lancaster LOVETT, dec. Wit: William PORTEN, John
MOSELEY.
    1DB6   9 Sep 1691:   George FOWLER grandson of
John SIDNEY confirms deed of 4 Jan 1648 to John
PORTER, Sr. and John PORTER, Jr. never recorded
of 300 acres. Wit: Mary KAVENING, Thomas SOLLEY.
    1DB10   13 Mar 1691:   John KELLEE of Anaran-
dall Co, MD power of attorney to brother-in-law
Benoni BURROUGH to acknowledge deed of sale to Hugh
HOPKINS. Wit: William BURROUGH, Richard LEE.
    1DB10   12 Nov 1691:   Solomon WHITE of Knotts
Island deed of gift to sister Elizabeth now wife
of Stephen SWAINE, 454 acres bounded by land of
father Patrick WHITE, dec. Wit: Patrick WHITE,
Patrick ANGUS.
    1DB11   15 Nov 1689: John RICHASON and Ann his
wife to Thomas WETHERING 200 acres granted Elizabeth
KEELING who married Thomas FICKLEY. Wit: Francis
SAYER, Thomas COOPER.
    1DB11   7 Oct 1691:   Thomas LOVETT acknowledges
receipt from his father-in-law James KEMPE of his
part of the estate left by his father Lancaster
LOVETT, dec. Wit: Benoni BURROUGHS, Thomas IVEY.
    1DB11   5 Oct 1691:   Inventory of the estate of
Patrick WHITE by John SANDFORD, Thomas JACKSON,
James DAUGE, Edward JONES sworn to by Elizabeth
WHITE, Admnx.
    1DB15   28 Dec 1691:   John PORTER, Sr. deed of
gift to the children of Thomas SOLLEY and my daugh-
ter Mary his wife - John, Thomas and Mary. Wit:
Thomas SCOTT, John PORTER, Jr.

1DB15 9 Jan 1691/2: William CORNICK to wife Alice's children Lemuell IVY and Aliffe IVY, sons-in law Ludford IVY and Anthony IVY.

1DB16 16 Jan 1691/16 Feb 1690/1: Thomas SKEVINGTON - Wester BEASHER, sister Elizabeth. Ex: John SANDFORD and Col. Anthony LAWSON. Wit: Edward NORWOOD, Edward BERRY.

1DB18 9 Mar 1691: William CORNICK to son Joell CORNICK tract called Black Walnutt Neck given to son William who died without issue - bordering land given by me to my daughter Barbra, wife of Capt. Francis MORSE. Wit: John RICHASON, John SANDFORD.

1DB19 7 May 1692: Francis LAND, father of Francis LAND and grandfather to Edward LAND, in his will dated 15 Apr 1654 left his son Francis 150 acres; eldest son Renatus LAND, father of Edward was to have 200 acres adjoining; Renatus died and land reverted to brother Francis who now gives to Edward. Wit: Malachy THRUSTON, Martha THRUSTON, Jean PORTEN.

1DB19 6 May 1692: John THOROWGOOD deed of gift to daughters Ann and Elizabeth. Wit: Edward MALLERY, William MALLERY, Jr.

1DB19 6 Jan 1689: Margaret FRISSELL, widow of Daniel FRISSELL, deed of gift to Daniel FRISSELL son of John FRISSELL, dec. Wit: Robert WANNERY, Robert ADAMS.

1DB20 ---/11 May 1692: John AVERY - wife and two daughters, son-in-law John RISIN. Wit: Henry FITZGERALD, Elenor SMITH.

1DB20 22 Mar 1691/2: Inventory of estate late in possession of Richard SMITH belonging to Ruth, orphan of William OAKHAM, dec. by Martin CORNICK, William CAPPS, Edward COOPER, John LA-BRITTOONE.

1DB20 10 May 1692: Elizabeth WHITE power of attorney to son Solomon WHITE. Wit: Evan JONES, Edward JONES.

1DB20 12 May 1692: Inventory of the estate of Richard SMITH by Robert WANNERY, Robert ADAMS.

1DB21 6 Jul 1692: Solomon WHITE, eldest son and heir of Patrick WHITE - it was father's desire that my brother Patrick WHITE have 350 acres called Indian Creek Woods and 200 acres in Norfolk Co. on the North River. Wit: Lemuell PHILLIPS, Patrick ANGUS.

1DB22 ---/6 Jul 1692: William HARFORD - noncupative will - son Malachy, wife. Wit: Joseph GOODAKER, John BIBBERY.

1DB22 6 Jul 1692: Elizabeth HARFORD deed of gift to son Malachy. Wit: John BEEBURY, Joell MARTIN, William CAPPS.

1DB23   6 Jul 1692:   Thomas JACKSON to wife Sarah, relict of Peter MALBONE, her estate inherited from Peter MALBONE - bond given to Peter son of Peter MALBONE. Wit: Francis SAYER, Lemuell PHILLIPS.

1DB23   24 May 1692:   Inventory of John AVERRY by William MOSELEY, Jr., Richard PLUMTON sworn to by Extrx Elizabeth AVERRY.

1DB24   11 Jul 1692:   Inventory of William WARFORD by William MOSELEY, Jr., Lancaster LOVETT, Lemuell PHILLIPS, William SMITH sworn to by Elizabeth WARFORD.

1DB26   6 Sep 1692:   Matthew BRINSON and Martha his wife sold land to John FRISSELL who died and bequeathed it to son Daniel - confirm unto Daniel FRISSELL 100 acres known as Long Ridge. Wit: Thomas COOPER, Patrick ANGUS.

1DB27   7 Sep 1692: William CORNICK and wife Alice, widow and extrx of Capt. Thomas Viz. IVY give power of attorney to Capt. Hugh CAMPBELL for collecting debts due IVY in MD. Wit: Benoni BURROUGH, Francis MORSE.

1DB27   18 Jul 1692:   Division of estate of Capt. Henry WOODHOUSE as given by will in order for Horatio WOODHOUSE to have his portion; Henry and Horatio take their parts; three youngest children John, Elizabeth and Lucy. Wit: William CORNICK, Robert RICHMOND, James LAMOUNT, Patrick ANGUS.

1DB28   27 Aug 1692:   Inventory of the estate of William OAKHAM in possession of Richard SMITH taken by James LAMOUNT, Patrick ANGUS, William OAKEHAM.

1DB28   2 Nov 1692:   Joell MARTIN son of John MARTIN, dec. to Adam KEELING 250 acres called the Great Plantation. Wit: Alexander KEELING, Henry WOODHOUSE.

1DB29   20 Sep 1692:   Argall THOROWGOOD deed of gift to daughter Frances which he had by deceased wife Pembroke given daughter by her grandfather LtCol. Adam THOROWGOOD - empower brothers Capt. John THOROWGOOD and Adam THOROWGOOD and cousin William MOSELEY to see deed performed. Wit: Edward MOSELEY, Sr., William MOSELEY, Jr.

1DB30   14 Dec 1692:   Isabella SPRATT, widow of Henry SPRATT and eldest son Henry SPRATT to Lancaster LOVETT 200 acres in the Western Shore. Wit: Job KEMPE, William BRADFORD, Francis SIMPSON.

1DB31   4 Jan 1692:   William MOSELEY, Jr. and John MOSELEY - our grandfather John GOOKIN left land to his only daughter Mary who married our father William MOSELEY and is now wife of Col. Anthony LAWSON - now divide 640 acres. Wit: Lemuell PHILLIPS, Mathew GODFREY, James PETERS.

1DB34   3 May 1693: John and Hannah JAMES deed
of gift of 100 acres to daughter Mary, wife of Robert LEWIS. Wit: James DAUGE, John JAMES, Jr.

1DB34   5 Apr 1692/3 May 1693: Elizabeth WHITE
of Knotts Island - daughters Dinah JONES, Elizabeth
SWAINE, Ruth WHITEALL; sons Solomon and Patrick.
Wit: William BOGGS, John SULLIVAN, John SANDFORD.

1DB35   3 May 1693: Joseph WALSTON died seized
of a plantation called Piney Island; William WAL-
STON being only heir sells to James PETERS for 2000
lbs. tobacco. Wit: Adam THOROWGOOD, George SMYTH.

1DB38   22 May 1692/3: Inventory of estate of
John SANDFORD, dec. by William CAPPS, Thomas FRICK-
LEY, James LAMOUNT and Adam HAYES sworn to by widow
Sarah SANDFORD.

1DB38   5 Jul 1693: Isabella SPRATT, widow of
Henry SPRATT, deed of gift to son Thomas of 300
acres upon Coratuck Bay called Nawney's Creek; if
he dies without issue then to son Henry. Wit:
Malachy THRUSTON, Francis SAYER, Otho RUSSELL.

1DB39   5 Jan 1692/3: John THOROWGOOD to John
MONTCREEF for 6000 lbs. tobacco 140 acres on the
west side of Samuel Bennett's Creek which belonged
to father LtCol. Adam THOROWGOOD commonly known as
Timber Nick and divided between me and my brothers
Argall, Adam, Francis and Robert. Wit: Edward MOSE-
LEY, Sr., Thomas IVY, William BURROUGH.

1DB40   5 Jul 1693: LtCol. Anthony LAWSON formerly sold 1250 acres to Capt. Adam KEELING, and
not having yet given him the deed now sells it to
his daughter Ann KEELING; in the event she dies
without issue then to her brothers Adam and Thomas.
Wit: Henry WOODHOUSE, Sarah SANDFORD, John RICHASON.

1DB41   27 May 1693: Thomas LOVETT gives power
of attorney to brother Lancaster LOVETT. Wit: Otho
RUSSELL, John CARRAWAY.

1DB41   6 Sep 1693: Isabella SPRATT, widow of
Henry, and son Henry trade 300 acres to daughter
Isabella now wife of Francis SIMPSON. Wit: Malachy
THRUSTON, Thomas HALL.

1DB43   6 Sep 1693: Anthony LAWSON to son-in-
law Edward MOSELEY and wife Frances for 12 lbs.
sterling half of 350 acres; other half to go to
son Anthony LAWSON. Wit: John FULCHER, William
MOSELEY, Jr., Richard LESTER.

1DB43   8 Aug 1693: Randolph LOVETT to Robert
CARTWRIGHT - whereas father Lancaster LOVETT bequeathed 800 acres to my brothers Lancaster, John
and Thomas; brother John died without issue and so
sells his portion for 6000 lbs. pork. Wit: Benoni
BURROUGH, Malachy THRUSTON.

1DB45 24 Apr 1693/6 Sep 1693: John WOODHOUSE-
eldest son John, son Henry; wife Ruth; daughters
Ruth FULCHER, Mary, Judith, Grace and Dinah; granddaughter Ruth OAKEHAM. Ex: wife. Wit: Jonas CHAPPLE,
Thomas BEDNAM, Patrick ANGUS.

1DB46 6 Sep 1693: Inventory of the estate of
John MEERIS by Mathew PALLETT, Lancaster LOVETT,
John KEMP and George POOLE sworn to by Ann MEARES.

1DB46 13 May 1693: Inventory of the estate
of William PRICE by Thomas WILKETS, Francis JONES,
Henry SOUTHERN, George WARRINGTON sworn to by Jane
PRICE.

1DB47 13 Nov 1693: Adam KEELING sells land
formerly belonging to John MARTIN which went to his
oldest son John MARTIN who died intestate so it
went to my mother Ann, widow of Capt. Adam KEELING
now wife of John RICHASON who gave it to son Adam
KEELING who now sells it to uncle Alexander KEELING
the Great Plantation. Wit: Adam THOROWGOOD, Adam
HAYES.

1DB48 6 Dec 1693: Henry WOODWARD to Lt. Adam
THOROWGOOD land Owen HAYES bequeathed to his son-
in-law and my father Francis WOODWARD who bequeathed
it to his eldest son John who died and it went to
Henry, 150 acres for 4000 lbs. tobacco. Wit: Malachy
THRUSTON, Francis SAYER, Alexander KEELING.

1DB49 18 Oct 1692/3 Jan 1693/4: George MIN-
CHIN - John and Thomas CANNON who now live with me;
Thomas FRICKLEY other half of plantation after the
death of my wife. Ex: wife Susana. Wit: Katherine
LAMOUNT, Robert HANNEY.

1DB50 3 Jan 1693/4: Mathew and Mary BRINSON
to brother John 100 acres in Dam Nick called Brushe
Ridge. Wit: Francis MORSE, Patrick ANGUS.

1DB52 6 Nov 1693/6 Dec 1693: Robert HARPER -
wife Sarah; sons John and James; daughter Mary - if
she dies without heirs then to John and Thomas COCK-
ROFT. Ex: wife, friends Lancaster LOVETT, James
THELABALL, James LAMOUNT and William MOSELEY, Jr.
to be overseers. Wit: William MOSELEY, Jr., Dennis
CARTEE, Richard LESTER, Hugh HOSKINS.

1DB55 20 Apr 1689/7 Mar 1693/4: Richard DRAPER-
wife Lucy; Richard DRAPIER, Jr. and his sisters Jane
and Mary. Overseers Charles HEATH, Thomas WILLEY.

1DB55 29 Apr 1693: Administration of the
estate of Patrick WHITE granted to Elizabeth WHITE,
relict.

1DB55 29 Apr 1693: Administration of the estate of John SANDFORD granted Sarah SANDFORD, relict.

1DB55 29 Apr 1693: Administration of the estate of Samuel MARSHALL granted Edward ATWOOD as
greatest creditor.

1DB55 28 Apr 1693: Administration of the estate of William HARFORD granted Elizabeth HARFORD,
relict.

1DB55 29 Apr 1693: Administration of the estate of John AVERY granted Elizabeth AVERY, relict.

1DB57 16 Dec 1693/3 May 1694: Margaret FRIS-SELL - sons of Adam HAYES Adam and Humphrey and Ketherine HAYES daughter of the aforesaid HAYES. Ex: Adam HAYES. Wit: Robert HANNEY, Richard COX, Anne KEELING.

1DB57 16 Apr 1694: Lawrance DAWLEY power of attorney to wife Jane while gone from Virginia. Wit: Edward COOPER, Richard BIRK, Ann BIRK.

1DB58 1 Oct 1692/4 Jul 1694: Michaell FENTRIS to daughter Rebecca SHOWLAND wife of John SHOWLAND, deed of gift of 50 acres. Wit: Thomas IVY, Thomas SOLLEY.

1DB58 3 Jul 1694: Johanna PURDY widow of James PURDY deed of gift to brother-in-law Thomas PURDY of 562 acres. Wit: Thomas WALKER, Job BROOKS, Patrick ANGUS.

1DB59 3 Jul 1694: Thomas PURDY to brother William PURDY 100 acres of the above land. Wit: Thomas WALKER, Job BROOKS, Patrick ANGUS.

1DB59 4 Jul 1694: John and Elizabeth BROOKS to sister Sarah AIRES 40 acres given by my father John. Wit: Wit: George WALKER, Evan JONES.

1DB59 4 Jul 1694: Job BROOKS to sister Sarah AIRES now wife of John AIRES deed of gift of 40 acres given me by my father John BROOKS. Wit: Joell CORNICK, William CAPPS.

1DB60 ---/4 Jul 1694: William LEVINGSTONE - noncupative will - sister Mary SMITH and brother John SMITH; father-in-law Richard SMITH. Wit: Charles KINSE, Elizabeth BROCK.

1DB61 ---/4 Jul 1694: William CARY - noncu-pative will - all to wife Elizabeth. Wit: William WALSTONE, Jr., Charles KENSEY.

1DB61 3 Feb 1693/4 Jan 1693/4: Thomas PURVINE - father Lewis, brothers Lewis and Joseph. Ex: father. Wit: William HUNTER, William DICKSON.

1DB61 23 Feb 1686/7/3 May 1694: William ED-WARDS - wife Elizabeth, sons Henry and Charles; daugh-ters Sarah and Martha. Ex: wife. Wit: James MULLI-GAN, Joseph BURIES, Thomas SOLLEY, John EDWARDS.

1DB61 25 Jun 1694/4 Jul 1694: John VAUGHAN - grandchildren Elizabeth, William, Anne and Benjamin CUMINGS, Jr. Ex: Thomas TOOLEY and Thomas WALKER. Wit: Adam FERGUSON, William CATON, Francis JONES.

1DB61 23 Jun 1694: Inventory of the estate of Richard LESTER by Adam THOROWGOOD, Lancaster LOVETT, George POOLE, Henry WALSTONE sworn to by wife Isabell.

1DB62 4 Jul 1694: Thomas RUSSELL of Penton in County Devon, mariner, now of Virginia power of attor-ney to son Otho. Wit: Mary RUSSELL, Jr. John MUNCREEF.

1DB64 5 Sep 1694: George and Frances NEWTON to Capt. Francis MORSE 200 acres called Surry Plantation

which I bought of Thomas GRIFFIN, formerly given to
Mary RUSSELL late wife of William HILLYARD by her
brother William WALSTONE and sold to me 16 Sep 1689
and land formerly belonging to William BASNETT and
sold to William SHREEFES and by will to his wife now
wife of Thomas MOORE and sold to me 16 Mar 1691 for
200 lbs. sterling and another tract called Piney
Island. Wit: Francis SAYER, Joell CORNICK, Malachy
THRUSTON.

1DB66 12 Mar 1693/4: Inventory of the estate
of Adam BOUTWELL by William HILLYARD, William MOORE,
Thomas FRANKLIN and Lawrence DAWLEY sworn to by
Mary BOUTWELL.

1DB66 8 Aug 1694: Inventory of the estate of
John VAUGHAN by Evan JONES, James DAUGE and Richard
BONNEY sworn to by Thomas WALKER, Ex.

1DB67 20 Mar 1693/4: Inventory of the estate
of Thomas FRICKLEY by Thomas RUSSELL, William CAPPS,
Adam HAYES and Edward OLD sworn to by Elizabeth
FRICKLEY alias MALBONE.

1DB68 5 Sep 1694: Appraisal of the estate of
John HOPKINS at the house of Hannah HOPKINS by
Richard BONNEY, Josias MORRIS, Thomas ETHERINGTON
and John BROWN.

1DB68 11 Jan 1695/5 Sep 1694: John GURNTO -
Peter son of William; brother William; Mary and
Elizabeth daughters of William. Ex: brother. Wit:
Richard BONNEY, John MOY.

1DB68 ---/5 Sep 1694: Thomas BARSLEY - land
to be equally divided between daughter Margaret and
child not born. Ex: wife. Wit: Charles HARTLEY,
Ursula HENLEY.

1DB71 21 May 1694: Inventory of the estate
of Thomas JACKSON by Richard BONNEY, Thomas NETHER-
INGTON, Josias MORRIS and James HEATH sworn to by
Sarah JACKSON.

1DB72 7 Nov 1694: Inventory of the estate of
William BARSLEY by Lancaster LOVETT, Henry WALSTON,
John HARRISON and Thomas HALL sworn to by Anne BAR-
SLEY alias BUTLER.

1DB72 7 Nov 1694: James LAMOUNT deed of gift
of 100 acres to daughter Katherine now wife of John
MACKIE. Wit: Benoni BURROUGH, James DAUGE.

1DB73 15 Oct 1694: Jane PRICE relct of William PRICE for 800 lbs. tobacco 100 acres to John
SEELY. Wit: Patrick ANGUS. Mary ANGUS.

1DB75 2 Jan 1694/5: Inventory of the estate
of Francis LAND by John RICHASON, Adam KEELING,
Henry WALSTON and William CATHRILL sworn to by
Katherine HALL late widow of Francis LAND.

1DB75 2 Jan 1694/5: Sarah JACKSON widow of
Thomas JACKSON appoints son John MALBONE power of
attorney. Wit: Titus EDWARDS, Thomas CREED, Sr.,
Thomas CREED, Jr.

1DB75   2 Jan 1694:   Mary HILLYARD deed of gift
to son Thomas RUSSELL. Wit: Matthew BRINSON, Thomas
HALL.

1DB75   6 Feb 1694/5:   Thomas FRANKLIN deed of
gift to son William FRANKLIN. Wit: Edward OLD, Jr.
Henry FITZGERALD.

1DB78   5 Feb 1694/5:   Sarah SANDFORD deed of
gift to sons Causon and Henry SANDFORD. Wit: Edward
ATWOOD, Horatio WOODHOUSE.

1DB78   5 Feb 1694/5:   Sarah SANDFORD power of
attorney to brother Henry WOODHOUSE. Wit: Horatio
WOODHOUSE, William MOORE.

1DB78   21 Jun 1694/6 Feb 1694/5:   John SIVIL -
wife Martha, son John, daughter Martha. If children should die before they come of age then to
James DAUGE son of James DAUGE after wife dies.
Ex: wife. Wit: John LYBURN, James DAUGE.

1DB80   ---/15 Oct 1694:   John GODDARD - noncupative will - Katherine GASKINS alias LAND and her
two children. Wit: John HUNT, Elizabeth HUNT.

1DB81   27 Jul 1694:   Inventory of the estate
of Thomas RIDER by Robert SMITH and John EVANS sworn
to by Henry FITZGERALD.

1DB84   28 Jun 1694/11 Jul 1694:   William HILL-
YARD - wife Mary, son and daughter-in-law William
and Anne RUSSELL. Ex: Capt. Abraham FRYFIELD and
Thomas BEARD, both of Barbados - in their absence
Henry WOODHOUSE and Lemuell PHILLIPS. Wit: Robert
BARKER, John SMITH, Samuel RICE, Thomas BROWN.

1DB87   5 Jun 1695:   Appraisal of the estate of
Thomas BARSLEY by Charles HENLY and Richard BONNEY
sworn to by Katherine BARSLEY WALKER.

1DB87   13 Dec 1694:   Esther SULLIVAN widow of
John SULLIVAN, Jr. power of attorney to father-in-
law John SULLIVAN. Wit: Thomas WEB, Patrick ANGUS.

1DB91   8 Jun 1695:   Capt. Francis MORSE deed
of gift to son Francis 360 acres adjacent to the
marshes of Knotts Island. Wit: William MOSELEY,
Jr., William HESLETT, Malachy THRUSTON.

1DB96   ---/3 Jul 1695:   William GRIFFIN - son
William. Ex: wife. Wit: William MILLER, Henry
COLLINS.

1DB97   17 Jun 1695:   Inventory of the estate of
William SHIPP by Tully EMPEROR, John KEMPE, Thomas
SOLLEY, George POOLE.

1DB98   28 Aug 1695:   Margaret ROBERTS power of
attorney to son Joseph to sell land belonging to
her and husband Samuel ROBERTS, Sr. Wit: Thomas
LAWSON, Godwin OUST.

1DB99   4 Sep 1695:   Richard WICKER of Knotts
Island to daughter Mary wife of George BOOTH 100
acres. Wit: Edward JONES, Richard DRAPER, Patrick
ANGUS.

1DB101   25 Jul 1695:   Francis THOROWGOOD of Somerset Co, MD power of attorney to brother Argall. Wit: Adam THOROWGOOD, Robert THOROWGOOD.

1DB103   6 Nov 1695:   James LAMOUNT deed of gift to son Edward 500 acres.   Wit: William MOSELEY, Jr., James DAUGE.

1DB104   6 Nov 1695:   Peter MALBONE and wife Elizabeth to brother John MALBONE one half of Long Island.   Wit: Joell CORNICK, Patrick ANGUS.

1DB105   9 Nov 1695:   Inventory of the estate of William HILLYARD sworn to by Mary GRANDY now wife of Thomas GRANDY late widow of William HILLYARD.

1DB107   15 Nov 1695:   John PORTER, Jr. of Chowan precinct in NC by power of attorney of John PORTER, Sr. sells to John ACKLES for 100 lbs. a parcel of land near the head of the Eastern Branch called Possum Quarter.   Wit: Richard WILLIAMSON, Henry BUTT, Thomas SOLLY.

1DB111   1 Jan 1695/6:   Anne BANKS deed of gift to son Thomas BANKS.

1DB111   14 Sep 1695/1 Jan 1695/6:   William HAMILTON, chirurgeon - Capt. William CRAFORD and his wife; two children of Nathan MCCLEHAND Andrew and William; three sisters living in Ireland - Jane wife of James HAMILTON, Jennit wife of William MCLENAHAN, and Ellen; John CORBITT.   Ex: William CRAFORD. Wit: Eliza ODEON, Alice TINSLEY, Thomas HODGES.

1DB113   21 Apr 1695:   Administration of John GODDARD granted Thomas HALL who married Katherine formerly wife of Job GASKINS and late wife of Francis LAND - her two children by GASKINS Job and Savill.

1DB113   21 Apr 1695:   Administration of William CARY granted Thomas BROCK who married his relict Elizabeth.

1DB115   1 Apr 1696:   Ruth WOODHOUSE deed of gift to children John, Henry, Judith, Grace, Dinah, Frances BOND and Ruth.   Wit: Benoni BURROUGH, Patrick ANGUS.

1DB116   2 Apr 1696:   Argall THOROWGOOD deed of gift to son Adam.

1DB116   1 Apr 1696:   John SHIRLEY deed of gift to son John.

1DB117   21 Apr 1695:   Administration of the estate of Pembroke THOROWGOOD alias FOWLER granted husband Argall THOROWGOOD.

1DB117   30 Mar 1695/6:   Thomas BROCK deed of gift to children John, James and Samuel.   Wit: Patrick ANGUS.

1DB118   16 Apr 1695/4 Mar 1695/6:   William ROBINSON - son Tully and after his death to his son William, grandson William SMITH, daughter Mary

THOROWGOOD, grandson William THOROWGOOD, daughter
Elizabeth SMITH wife of George SMITH. Ex: son Tully
and George SMITH. Wit: Sarah EMPEROR, William MOSE-
LEY, Jr., Lemuel PHILLIPS.

1DB120 11 Nov 1695/7 May 1696: Gilbert LEWIS-
wife Sarah, land to William COCKE after decease of
wife. Wit: Alexander KEELING, Adam KEELING.

1DB120 11 Apr 1696: Henry FITZGERALD and his
wife Mary to brother James FITZGERALD for 6000 lbs.
of pork 50 acres which belonged to my father Morris
FITZGERALD. Wit: Benoni BURROUGH, Lancaster LOVETT,
John HOSKINS.

1DB121 1 Jul 1696: Horatio and Lucy WOODHOUSE
daughter of Thorowgood KEELING, dec. to William MOORE
for 20000 lbs. tobacco 300 acres. Wit: Joell COR-
NICK, William HUNTER, Patrick ANGUS.

1DB121 14 Apr 1696/2 Jul 1696: John THROWER-
Extrx and heiress wife Alice. Wit: Sarah PETERS,
Rebekah ROBERTS.

1DB123 25 Apr 1696: Charles NEALE of NC sells
100 acres called Kendalls Island which wife Mary
heired from John WOODHOUSE. Wit: John WOODHOUSE,
Ruth SNAYLE.

1DB123 2 Sep 1696: Sarah HARPER deed of gift
to sons Jehue and Thomas COCKROFT sons of William
COCKROFT. Wit: Malachy THRUSTON, William MOSELEY,Sr.

1DB125 30 Jul 1696: Administration of the
estate of Francis SHIPP granted to son William SHIPP.

1DB125 30 Jul 1696: Administration of the
estate of William HILLYARD granted Thomas GRANDY
who married his relict Mary - two of her children
William and Anne RUSSELL.

1DB126 5 Nov 1696: Thomas HATTERSLEY only
heir of William HATTERSLEY to Col Anthony LAWSON
a tract of land in Little Creek for land in the
woods toward North River. Wit: Robert THOROWGOOD,
Mark POWELL, Thomas COCKE.

1DB127 5 Nov 1696: Col. Anthony LAWSON 350
acres to be divided equally between Thomas HATTERS-
LEY and my son-in-law Edward MOSELEY and Frances
his wife. Wit: Robert THOROWGOOD, Mark POWELL,
Thomas COCKE.

1DB127 5 Nov 1696: Francis BROCKETT and wife
Rebecka to Anthony LAWSON land wife inherited from
her father Joshua CORNWALL in Little Creek. Wit:
Edward MOSELEY, Sr., Robert THOROWGOOD, Mark POWELL.

1DB128 5 Nov 1696: Anthony LAWSON to Francis
BROCKETT 50 acres bought of Robert THROWGOOD young-
est son of Adam. Wit: Edward MOSELEY, Sr., Robert
THOROWGOOD, Mark POWELL.

1DB130 13 Dec 1693/4 Nov 1696: Elizabeth
HARBIN late of Barbados - sister Sarah LEE of

Barbados, cousin Miss RAMSEY daughter of Elizabeth
RAMSEY, cousin William son of Elizabeth RAMSEY,
Francis EMPEROR son of Francis EMPEROR and Sarah,
kinsman Tully ROBINSON. Ex: Sarah EMPEROR. Overseers: Thomas SHEARMOND and Joseph HOUGH of Barbados. Wit: George SMYTH, Tully ROBINSON, Francis
CHEETAM, Benjamin ROBERTS.

1DB131 6 May 1696: Thomas IVY son of Thomas
V. IVY and Ursula his wife to brothers Anthony,
Samuel and Lemuell. Wit: James KEMP, Patrick ANGUS.

1DB134 ---/6 Jan 1696/7: Edward COOPER -
sons Edward, John and Thomas; daughters Milbrough,
Sarah and Elizabeth; wife Milbrough. Ex: wife.
Wit: John BUCK, Richard BIRK, Lawrence DAWLEY.

1DB136 15 Oct 1694/6 May 1697: William ERVIN-
after decease of wife Katherine, estate to Anne COCKE
daughter of Capt. Thomas COCKE. Ex: wife. Wit:
John BROWN, Evan PERKINS, Thomas COCKE.

1DB138 ---/3 Mar 1696/7: John BASNITT - noncupative will - daughter Elizabeth and sister Mary.
Wit: Lewis PURVINE, Mary HIDE.

1DB138 ---/3 Mar 1696/7: John BROWN - noncupative will - all to wife Elizabeth. Wit: John
RICHASON, Owen MAGRAVY.

1DB138 8 Aug 1694/5 May 1697: William CAPPS-
sons William, John and Joell; daughters Ruth, Elizabeth, Sarah, Mary; wife Frances. Ex: wife. Wit:
William CORNICK, Martin CORNICK.

1DB139 ---/5 May 1697: Richard HAMILTON -
noncupative will - all to Robert RENNEY. Wit:
John PITTS, Edward TURTON.

1DB142 8 Jan 1694/5/7 Jul 1697: James JOUSLIN-
son Richard, wife Elizabeth. Overseers Edward MOSE-
LEY, Sr. and Henry CHAPMAN. Wit: Ann CHAPMAN, John
SMITH, James THELABALL, Edward MOSELEY, Sr.

1DB142 15 Apr 1697/7 Jul 1697: Jeffery BECK-
son Edward, daughters Elizabeth and Anne, wife Elizabeth. Ex: wife. Wit: John HARISON, Adam HAYES.

1DB144 22 Feb 1696/7: Frances CAPPS power
of attorney to brother Richard COX to obtain probate
of late husband William CAPPS. Wit: Owen SULLIVAN,
Patrick ANGUS.

1DB145 ---/7 Jul 1697: John RUSSELL - wife
Elizabeth and daughter Elizabeth. Ex: wife. Wit:
Thomas SPRATT, Josias MORRIS, Samuell HANCOCK.

1DB146 16 Jun 1697: Administration of the
estate of Gilbert LEWIS granted Mathew PALLETT who
married relict Sarah.

1DB151 ---/7 May 1700: John EVANS - noncupative will - wife Elizabeth and son John. Wit: John
CAVENER, Thomas OWENS.

1DB152 1 Sep 1697: Thomas HERISON to brother Henry - land deceased brother John wanted him to have. Wit: William CORNICK, Patrick ANGUS.

1DB153 6 Oct 1697: John SALMON and wife Elizabeth 150 acres to brother William SALMON. Wit: Elizabeth MACLANAHAN, John OAKHAM.

1DB154 20 Aug 1697/6 Oct 1697: Thomas COCKE - daughters Anne and Mary, cousin Christopher COCKE, cousin John and Mary BOLITHO, brothers Walter and William. Ex: Walter and William, Thomas COCKE, Thomas MASON and Christopher COCKE. Wit: Edward MOSELEY, Sr., George SMYTH, John BOLITHO.

1DB154 17 Feb 1696/7/6 Oct 1697: John WHARTON- Anne SEELY late wife of John SEELY, William KEATON. Ex: Anne SEALLY. Wit: Anthony LAWSON, James LAMOUNT, Benoni BURROUGH.

1DB155 ---/6 Oct 1697: John HARRISON - non- cupative will - brother Thomas, sister James WARDEN, brother Henry, sister Susanna. Wit: Margaret SIM- MONS, Elizabeth BECK.

1DB157 29 Nov 1697: Thomas and Abiah TOOLY deed of gift to Edward OLD, Jr. who married my daugh- ter Rebecca, 100 acres called Poplar Neck. Wit: Christopher MERCHANT, Abiah MERCHANT.

1DB158 20 Oct 1697/1 Dec 1697: John HOSKINS - wife Ann, brother Richard, father and mother Hugh and Dorcas HOSKINS, sister Mary. Wit: William MOSE- LEY; Jr., Robert THOROWGOOD, Richard CORBITT.

1DB159 4 Jan 1693/4/7 Oct 1697: Thomas WEBB - Henry WOODHOUSE, Henry FITZGERALD. Ex: Henry WOOD- HOUSE. Wit: Dennis MCCARTY, Henry FITZGERALD.

1DB170 4 Feb 1697/8: Richard DROUT, Sr. deed of gift to son Richard DROUT, Jr. a parcel of land provided he pay his sister Elizabeth 2000 lbs. when she marries or comes of age. Wit: Francis SAYER, Richard CORBETT.

1DB170 5 Jan 1697/8: Alice GIBSON deed of gift to son-in-law John MAYO. Wit: Otho RUSSELL, Thomas RUSSELL.

1DB172 28 Feb 1697/8: William SIMMONS and wife Mary to brother Henry SIMMONS for 1800 lbs. tobacco 100 acres. Wit: Thomas WALKER, Francis JONES.

1DB173 1 Feb 1697/8/2 Mar 1697/8: Lewis PUR- VINE - sons Joseph, Richard, John and Lewis; daughter Mary. Ex: son Lewis. Wit: Jonas CHAPPEL, Edward BAKER, James DAUGE.

1DB174 23 Oct 1697/2 Mar 1697/8: Benjamin CUMMINGS - sons William, Benjamin and John. Ex: wife. Wit: Thomas BERRY, William SIMMONS, Henry SIMMONS.

1DB177 5 May 1698: James GUY and wife Mary, one of the daughters and coheirs of Thomas WORKMAN

heir of John WORKMAN, to Robert HUMPHREY. Wit:
Robert RICHMOND, Mark POWELL, Patrick ANGUS.
 1DB180 31 Jan 1697/8/5 May 1698: Capt.
Thomas RUSSELL - sons Otho and Daniell. Ex: Otho.
Wit: Edward CANNON, Thomas CANNON, Mary BOUTWELL.
 1DB180 13 Mar 1697/8/4 May 1698: Elizabeth
EDWARDS - son John SALMON, daughter Susan BURIES,
grandson Renatus LAND, son Charles EDWARDS, daughters Sarah and Martha EDWARDS, daughter Mary SAL-
MON, son William SALMON. Ex: William SALMON. Wit:
George SMITH, Mary MOORE, Thomas SOLLEY.
 1DB181 26 Nov 1704: Administration of the
estate of John BIGGS granted relict Eleanor.
 1DB182 28 Nov 1706: Administration of the
estate of William GRINTO granted relict Mary.
 1DB185 6 Jul 1698: Elinor WILLY deed of gift
to son Richard WILLY. Wit: John EDWARDS, Richard
WILLIAMS.
 1DB186 2 Jul 1695/6 Jul 1698: Owen WILLY -
son Owen, daughters Anne, Mary, Elanor, Sarah and
Elizabeth; wife Elinor. Ex: wife. Wit: Richard
WILLIAMSON, John GODFREY, Jr., William SHIP, John
EDWARDS.
 1DB92 7 Sep 1698: William SHIPP deed to brother John SHIPP 100 acres called the Cyprus Neck.
Wit: Joseph EDWARDS, Edward WOOD.
 1DB192 6 Sep 1698: William GRANT deed of
gift to daughter Isabell. Wit: Patrick ANGUS, Mary
ANGUS.
 1DB193 25 Jul 1698/7 Sep 1698: Bartholomew
WILLIAMSON - son Charles, son James land bought of
brother-in-law William CHRISTOPHER, wife Martha,
daughter Sarah wife of Thomas HARYSON, daughter
Mary widow of Francis BOND, daughter Elizabeth wife
of Thomas SPRATT, daughter Martha, grandson Bartholomew son of Francis BOND. Ex: wife and Charles.
Overseers: Benoni BURROUGH, Edward MOSELEY, Sr.and
brother Richard. Wit: Edward MOSELEY, Sr., William
MOSELEY, Sr., Thomas HARISON, Francis MOSELEY.
 1DB194 12 May 1698/7 Sep 1698: John SULLIVAN-
sons Owen and Morris, daughter Honor wife of Richard
COX, daughter Mary wife of Patrick ANGUS, daughters
Amie and Anne, wife Sarah, grandson John SULLIVAN.
Ex: son-in-law Patrick ANGUS. Wit: George MARSH,
William BROCK, Jr.
 1DB199 8 Sep 1698: Inventory and appraisement
of estate of Lawrence DAWLEY by Otho RUSSELL, Horatio
WOODHOUSE, John KEELING, Joseph WHITE.
 1DB201 2 Nov 1698: Richard BONNEY and wife
Mary to son-in-law and daughter Thomas and Sarah
FRANKLIN 150 acres. Wit: John MACKIE, Thomas IVY.

1DB203   7 Dec 1698: Deposition of Mary LOVE
wife of Timothy LOVE that her husband set sail for
England in Jun 1696 and never returned.

1DB206   3 Jan 1698/9: William WALSTONE to
brother Joseph land their father William wanted him
to have - 100 acres, part of 450 acres granted to
grandfather Thomas WALSTONE. Wit: Anne WARDLEY,
Patrick ANGUS, Mary ANGUS.

1DB207   31 Oct 1698: Job BROOKS to James WIL-
LIAMS for 2500 lbs. tobacco 70 acres, being part
of patent granted my father John BROOKS. Wit:
Richard WATERMAN, John HENLY.

1DB215   27 Feb 1698/9: George SMYTH makes
son William his power of attorney. Wit: Thomas
SOLLEY, Henry MIDDLETON.

1DB215   6 Nov 1698/1 Mar 1698/9: Christopher
MERCHANT - son-in-law Thomas TOOLEY, daughter Abiah
TOOLEY, son Willoby MERCHANT, wife Abiah. Ex: wife.
Wit: William ALLEN, Nathaniel TOMS, Henry NEWMAN.

1DB216   16 Jul 1698/1 Mar 1698/9: Francis
BOND - sons Robert, Bartholomew and Francis. Ex:
wife Mary. Wit: Edward ATTWOOD, Edward OLD, Rachell
BENSON.

1DB220   3 May 1699: Division of property of
Henry WOODHOUSE - Joell CORNICK and wife Elizabeth
daughter of WOODHOUSE pay Lucy her share. Wit:
William CORNICK, James LAMOUNT, John RICHASON,
Patrick ANGUS.

1DB223   4 Jul 1699: Anne WARDLEY daughter of
Owen HAYES who gave 200 acres to John SULLIVAN who
died and it reverted to heirs, gives 50 acres to
cousin Morris SULLIVAN. Wit: James MACARTY, William
SMITH, Patrick ANGUS.

1DB224   4 Jul 1699: William RICHASON to son
Roger WILLIAMSON 100 acres. Wit: John EDWARDS,
Bartholomew WILLIAMSON.

1DB225   27 Mar 1699/7 Jul 1699: Capt. William
MOSELEY, Jr. son of William, dec. - Malachy son of
William HARPER and Elizabeth his wife and Florintis
son of James and Mary PORTER who were godsons of my
wife Blandina, dec., daughters Mary and Elizabeth,
sons William and Richard (formerly his grandfather
POOLE's), two fathers-in-law Col. Anthony LAWSON
and Maj. Francis SAYER, brothers Edward and John,
sisters Margaret THOROWGOOD and Elizabeth LAWSON,
Josias MACKIE, children of my brother WALKE and
Mary his wife. Ex: wife Elizabeth. Wit: Edward
MOSELEY, Jr., Thomas HATTERSLY, Phil PIGHTLING.

1DB229   4 Sep 1699: Michael FENTRIS deed to
daughter Mary. Wit: John EDWARDS.

1DB229   5 Sep 1699:   Lemuel MASON, Sr. and wife Anne appoint son Thomas power of attorney. Wit: George MASON, Lemuel MASON, Jr.

1DB233   2 Nov 1699:   Elizabeth RICHMOND deed of gift to her children Nathaniel BARKER, Anthony RICHMOND, Amie RICHMOND and John RICHMOND.   Wit: Francis SAYER, Patrick ANGUS.

1DB233   29 Sep 1694/1 Nov 1699:   John LEGGETT-wife; sons John, David and Alexander.   Ex: wife. Wit: Michaell JONES, George BOOTH.

1DB244   12 Aug 1699/1 May 1700:   Daniell LANE-wife Elizabeth.   Ex: wife.   Wit: W. ORCHARD, Stephen SALS, Lucy SALLS.

1DB245   5 Mar 1699/1700:   William WISHART to brother Thomas 100 acres left me by our father James. Wit: Henry CHAPMAN, Hester CHAPMAN.

1DB246   7 May 1700:   Daniel and John MAKEEL of Pasquotank in NC 100 acres patented by out father Derman MAKEEL for 5000 lbs. tobacco to Robert PETRIE. Wit: William CATERELL, Nathaniel MCCLANAHAN.

1DB247   25 Nov 1699/7 May 1700:   Argall THOROW-GOOD - wife Ann; sons Argall, William and Adam, daughters Elizabeth and Frances; unborn child.   Ex: wife. Wit: Robert PEALE, Robert THOROWGOOD, Thomas SOLLEY.

1DB251   8 Feb 1699/1700/7 May 1700:   Isabell SPRATT - son Henry and his wife Frances, daughter Amie, Sarah daughter of Henry WOODHOUSE and his wife Amie, son Thomas and his daughter Amy, daughter Mary wife of Solomon WHITE, daughter Isabel wife of Patrick WHITE, Col. Anthony LAWSON.   Ex: son Henry and son-in-law Henry WOODHOUSE.   Wit: Edward MOSELEY, Henry CHAPMAN.

1DB254   1 Jul 1700:   Major Francis SAYER deed of gift to daughter Mary THOROWGOOD.   Wit: Patrick ANGUS.

1DB256   18 Apr 1700/3 Jul 1700:   Adam BELLENY-son Adam; daughters Jane, Mary and Elizabeth; wife. James WISHART and Walter JONES to be overseers. Brother Simon FRANKLIN to have the disposing of my two children.   Wit: Elizabeth JONES, Walter JONES.

1DB258   7 Nov 1700:   Mark POWELL deed of gift to daughters Sarah and Anne.   Wit: John COCKROFT, William GOODACRE.

1DB258   7 Nov 1700:   Nicholas WILLIS discharges father-in-law Edward DAVIS from father Nicholas WILLIS's estate.   Wit: William SMITH, Thomas SOLLEY.

1DB260   4 Nov 1700:   Edward DAVIS deed of gift to son-in-law Nicholas WILLIS 100 acres at head of Eastern Branch - if he dies to my son Thomas DAVIS. Wit: John MUNCREEF, Henry CHAPMAN.

1DB261   7 Nov 1700:   Peter MALBONE gift to son Godfrey.   Wit: Richard CORBITT, Tully SMITH.

1DB261   7 Nov 1700: John WOODHOUSE, Sr. to brother Horatio land called George Quarter left me by my father Henry. Wit: John RICHASON, Henry COLLINS.

1DB261   ---/31 Jan 1699/1700: Thomas CANNON - brother John, cousin Edward CARRAWAY. Wit: Henry WOODHOUSE, Thomas COOPER, William WOODHOUSE.

1DB262   11 Ict 1699/7 Nov 1700: Bryan CAHILLE, taylor - John LAWN, Patrick CONDON, Thomas LAWSON, Mary STRINGER, Col. Anthony LAWSON. Ex: Col LAWSON. Wit: John THOROWGOOD, Edward MOSELEY, Sr., Mary BRYAN, Sarah ELDER.

1DB262   3 Oct 1700/7 Nov 1700: Robert HANNEY- son Josiah, 1 shilling apiece to those evil begotten children of my wife, nothing to wife. Ex: Horatio WOODHOUSE. Wit: Peter MALBONE, Alex WILLEY, John RICHASON.

1DB263   7 Sep 1700/6 Nov 1700: William COR- NICK - sons Martin, John and Joell; daughter Barbra MORSE wife of Capt. Francis MORSE; wife Alice; son Lemuel IVY. Ex: wife and son John. Wit: Henry WOODHOUSE, Horatio WOODHOUSE, John RICHASON, Benjamin DREWITT.

1DB267   21 Dec 1699: Administration of John BUCK granted to widow Anne BUCK.

1DB268   19 Sep 1700/2 Jan 1700: Edward COOPER- Sarah DYER daughter of William DYER, brother and sister. Ex: Thomas COOPER. Wit: William DYER, Thomas COOPER.

1DB268   23 Oct 1700/9 Jan 1700: George FOWLER- wife Mary, son George, daughter Francis and Pembrok. Ex: wife. Wit: William SMITH, Simon FRANKLIN, John EDWARDS.

1DB268   ---/9 Jan 1700: Dorothy RULEY - non- cupative will - all to Hugh HOSKINS. Wit: Benoni BURROUGH (55), Richard CORBETT (28)

1DB269   ---/16 Jan 1700: William BURROUGH - sons John and William, daughter Amy, daughter Mary TRIGGS. Ex: son John. Wit: John EDWARDS, Ither TRIGGS, Mary TRIGGS, William MOSELEY, Sr.

1DB270   12 Nov 1700/2 Jan 1700: Sarah JONES of Knotts Island - son John LEWIS, son William EVANS, John JONES. Ex: son William. Wit: Adam BROUGHTON, Samuell BERRIT, Ambros MCCOY.

1DB270   1 Jan 1700: Elizabeth LYBURNE deed of gift to son John RUSSELL that husband John RUSSELL wanted him to have. Wit: Thomas HALL, John HARPER.

1DB272   20 Nov 1700: Inventory of Patrick ANGUS by John RICHASON, James LAMAN and Horatio WOODHOUSE sworn to by Mrs. Mary ANGUS.

1DB274   21 Sep 1700/4 May 1700:   Thomas SOLLEY -
wife Francis, son John, daughter Elizabeth, son-in-
law Richard WICHALL, daughters Anne, Leda and Sarah,
daughter Mary. Ex: wife. Wit: James TURNDALL, Mary
RAVENING, Mary SMYTH, Richard CHURCH.

1DB276   7 Mar 1700:   Jacob JOHNSON deed of gift
to daughter Mary wife of James WISHARD - Hogge Island,
if no heirs to son Jacob. Wit: Simon ELDERSON, Nathaniel MCCLANAHAN.

1DB277   4 Mar 1701:   Elizabeth LANE deed of
gift to William HANNAH son to Catherine wife of
Robert HANNAH, dec. Wit: John RICHASON, Charles
KENSEY.

1DB277   4 Mar 1700/1:   Elizabeth LANE deed of
gift to Edward RIELY (or KILLEY). Wit: John RICHA-
SON, Alex WILLEY.

1DB277   8 Mar 1700:   Adam THOROWGOOD deed of
gift to Adam GOODACRE. Wit: Francis SAYER, Charles
SAYER.

1DB278   18 Nov 1684:   Francis SHIP and wife
Sarah deed of gift to John EVANS 100 acres at head
of North River. Wit: William MAUND, Michaell FEN-
TRES.

1DB278   14 Sep 1700/5 Mar 1700/1:   William
WOODHOUSE - sons Henry, John, Horatio and Francis;
daughters Sarah, Mary and Margaret. Ex: wife.
Wit: John BRINSON, John BULLER, Otho COOPER.

1DB280   9 Nov 1700:   Administration of the
estate of Matthew BRINSON granted relict Mary.

1DB280   21 Sep 1696/- May 1701:   Margaret DAW-
LEY - sons William CAPPS, Richard CAPPS and John
DAWLEY; daughters Jeane WOODHOUSE, Sarah CANNON,
Elizabeth JONES; Dennis CAPPS son of Henry; Sarah
CANNON daughter of Edward and Sarah; Francis JONES
and his sister Sarah. Ex: son John DAWLEY. Wit:
William SIMMONS, John WALKER.

1DB281   27 Jul 1691/10 Oct 1701:   Phillip PIGHT-
LING son of John PIGHTLING, John PIGHTLING great
Bible my godfather Col. Phillip HARBORD gave me,
sister Mary PIGHTLING, Ant Barbra MORSE, uncle
Francis MORSE. Ex: Francis MORSE. Wit: William
ALLEN, Richard DRAPER, John PLOWMAN.

1DB282   3 May 1701/2 Jul 1701:   Edward BAKER -
wife Elizabeth, father-in-law Lewis PURVINE's little girl Elizabeth BENSON. Wit: John WOODHOUSE,
Thomas BENSON, William WARREN, James CHAPPEL, William HUNTER.

1DB283   2 Mar 1700/2 Jul 1701:   Adam HAYES -
wife Elizabeth; sons Edward, Adam and Humphrey;
daughters Sarah, Catherine and Lucy. Ex: wife.
Wit: John MACKIE, Edward HAYES.

1DB283   3 Feb 1703/4:   Lemuell IVY - noncupative will - all to mother. Wit: John CORNICK (25), William CAPPS (23).

1DB284   4 Jan 1700/30 Jan 1700: Richard WICKER of Coratuck in NC - wife Margaret, two grandchildren George BOOTH, daughters Anne and Elizabeth, Robert LINSEY, sons John and Joseph. Ex: son William WICKER. Wit: Anne THOMAS, Peter PARKER, Nathaniel JAMES.

1DB284   13 Feb 1700/2 Jul 1700: Simon HANDCOCK, Sr - wife Susannah; sons George and William, daughters Mary, Elizabeth, Sarah and Dina. Ex: wife. Wit: Jacob JOHNSON, James WISHART, Gale COLLINS.

1DB285   17 Mar 1700/7 May 1701: Thomas MORRIS - wife Dorothy, daughter Mary, daughters Elizabeth and Dorcas wives to John BROWN and Thomas HATTERSLEY. Ex: wife. Wit: Edward MOSELEY, Bryant CAHILL, Edward MOSELEY, Sr.

1DB285   20 Nov 1700/7 May 1701: William BROCK - wife Sarah, Thomas BROCK son of John BROCK. Ex: wife. Wit: Joseph BENSON, Otho COOPER.

1DB286   16 Oct 1700/5 Mar 1700: Anne BECK - sons Jeremiah, Benjamin and George, daughter Hannah DOLLAR, daughter Anne EVERIDGE, daughter Margaret. Ex: Joseph DOLLAR and son James MCCOY. Wit: Christopher COCKE, Lemuell WILSON.

1DB287   2 Sep 1701: Sarah BROCK relict of William BROCK deed of gift to cousen Thomas KEATON son of William KEATON of Blackwater, cousen Jean KEATON daughter of William KEATON. Wit: Otho COOPER, Thomas BROCK, Jr.

1DB287   1 May 1701: Jane WOODHOUSE deed of gift to children Henry, Sarah, Mary and Margaret; cousin Sarah JONES daughter of Francis JONES (to sister Elizabeth if she dies); cousen Jane CANNON daughter of Edward CANNON, Sr. (to sister Sarah if she dies). Wit: Joell CORNICK.

1DB292   5 Nov 1701: Alice CORNICK deed of gift to son Lemuell IVY, grandson Thomas IVY son of son Thomas IVY - for want of heirs to his brother Anthony. Wit: John RICHASON, Cason MORE.

1DB292   8 Sep 1701: Benoni BURROUGHS and wife Mary to Lewis PURVINE for 3000 lbs. tobacco 200 acres on Eastern Shore of Linhaven River which formerly belonged to my uncle William BURROUGHS which my father Christopher BURROUGHS sold without any authority. Wit: John EDWARDS, Christopher BURROUGH.

1DB295   2 Oct 1701: John JAMES, Sr. and wife Hannah deed of gift to daughter Mary LEWIS wife of Richard LEWIS 100 acres. Wit: Thomas HALL, Henry WOODHOUSE.

1DB296   21 Sep 1701/5 Nov 1701:   Edward CANNON-
wife Mary, son John, daughter (100 acres given by
George MINSEY to John CANNON son of Thomas), child
wife goes with. Ex: wife. Wit: John CARRAWAY, Mary
RUSSELL, Otho RUSSELL.

1DB299   ---/16 Oct 1701: Francis HEWETT - noncupative will - sister Elizabeth EMPEROR, brother
John HEWETT. Wit: Mary FOWLER, James MCCOY.

1DB309   13 Jan 1701/2:   Elizabeth BROWNE widow
of John BROWNE deed of gift to sons Edward and John.
Wit: Joel CORNICK, James ANGUS.

1DB309   14 Jan 1701:   William MOORE deed of
gift to children Samuel, William, James and John.
Wit: Joel CORNICK, William SMITH.

1DB311   5 Mar 1700:   Peter MALBONE deed to
brother John 100 acres. Wit: Nathaniel MCCLANAHAN,
Thomas HALL.

1DB311   25 Apr 1701:   Richard SMITH deed of
gift to children-in-law John ASHBY, Sarah ASHBY,
Mary ASHBEE, Ann ASHBEE and Thomas ASHBEE (dec.
father William ASHBEE). Wit: Joell CORNICK, Elizabeth CORNICK, James ANGUS.

1DB312   9 Dec 1701/7 Jan 1701/2:   Col. John
THOROWGOOD - wife Margaret, sons Anthony and John,
daughters Ann and Elizabeth. Ex: wife. Wit: Edward MOSELEY, Sr., John MOSELEY, Sr., Abraham PLOMER.

1DB313   6 May 1702:   Thomas LAWSON coadminis-
trator of LtCol. Anthony LAWSON deed to cousins
John, Anthony and Margaret children of LtCol. John
THOROWGOOD. Wit: William MOSELEY, Sr., C. COCKE.

1DB316   13 Sep 1699:   John BROADHURST the
younger of London - wife Elizabeth, children Elizabeth, Ann, Thomas and John. Ex: wife. Overseer
cozen Roger BOTTON.

1DB318   8 May 1701:   Joseph DOLLAR deed of gift
to son James. Wit: John EDWARDS, George MOSELEY.

1DB318   18 Aug 1701/5 Mar 1701:   Robert SMITH-
wife Elinor, son James. Ex: wife and son. Wit:
Charles GRIFFEN, John GRIFFEN, Thomas GRIFFEN.

1DB323   6 May 1700:   Mary CANNON deed of gift
to son John and daughter Elizabeth. Wit: Mark POWELL,
John CARROWAY, Jr.

1DB328   13 Mar 1701/7 May 1702:   Thomas TOOLEY -
wife Abia: daughters Jane, Elizabeth, Mary and Rebecca OLD; son-in-law Edward OLD and William LEARY.
Wit: Thomas WALKER and William LURREY.

1DB332   ---/6 May 1702:   John BROWNE - noncupative will - sons John and Edward. Wit: James
GITTERY.

1DB333   2 Apr 1702/6 May 1702:   Richard ABRA-
HAM - John SEALY son of John SEALY, dec., Jeane
CATON daughter of William and Elizabeth CATON, Clif-
ton WARRENTON son of George, John YELKE, John son of

William CATON, Mary PRISE, William CATON, Sarah
SIMSON daughter of James SIMSON and Mary, Francis
NASH, Jr., Ann SEALY, Adam TOOLEY, John SIMSON,
Mary SIMSON, widow. Wit: Francis NASH, James TOOLEY.
    1DB335 2 Jul 1701: Administration of the es-
tate of John KEELING granted relict Ann.
    1DB335 8 May 1701: Administration of the es-
ate of Martin CORNICK granted Joell CORNICK.
    1DB338   Aug 1702: James and Elizabeth PETERS
deed of gift to nephew George HANDCOCK. Wit: William SMYTH, Tully SMITH.
    1DB339 ---/7 Mar 1701: John EVERIT - noncu-
pative will - Nathaniel BARBER, Anthony RICHMOND,
Thomas BENSON. Wit: Lewis PROVINE.
    1DB349 6 Jan 1702: William DYER son of Wil-
liam DYER and wife Sarah - father sold 200 acres
to Edward COOPER grandfather of John COOPER which
was escheated and patented in my name, to John COOPER,
cordwainer. Wit: John RICHASON, Joseph CHOICE.
    1DB351 ---/7 Jan 1702/3: Robert THOROWGOOD-
wife Dina, sons Thomas and Robert, daughter Priscilla. Ex: wife. Wit: Mark POWELL, John EDWARDS,
A. THOROWGOOD.
    1DB358 3 Mar 1702/3: Susanna HANDCOCK relict
of Simon and daughter of George ASHWELL deed of gift
to son Ashwell HANDCOCK 100 acres. Wit: William
SMYTH, Charles SAYER.
    1DB359 3 Mar 1702/3: Thomas LAWSON deed of
gift to children Frances, Anne, George and Anthony.
Wit: Christopher COCKE, Sampson TREVETHAN.
    1DB359 ---/3 Mar 1702/3: William DIXON -
noncupative will - Thomas KEELING son of Thomas,
wife Margery. Wit: John RICHASON, William LOVETT.
    1DB360 25 Oct 1700/3 Mar 1702/3: Lancaster
LOVETT - sons Lancaster, Thomas, Adam, William and
John; daughters Sarah and Elizabeth wife of Thomas
KEELING. Ex: wife Mary. Overseers: Adam THOROW-
GOOD, son-in-law Thomas KEELING, Thomas HARRISON
and son William. Wit: Thomas HERISON, Henry WALSTONE,
Robert CARTWRIGHT, John EDWARDS.
    1DB362 24 Jan 1702/3/5 May 1703: Thomas WALKER-
sons John and Thomas, wife Sarah, Thomas BEARSLEY.
Ex: wife. Wit: Edward OULD, Jr., Peter POYNER, John
SIMMONS, John JONES.
    1DB363 5 May 1703: Thomas LAWSON deed of gift
to son Anthony. Wit: Christopher COCKE, Robert PEALE,
John FULCHER.
    1DB363 5 May 1703: Thomas LAWSON deed of gift
to son George. Wit: Christopher COCKE, Robert PEALE,
John FULCHER.
    1DB364 29 Jun 1703: Thomas OWEN deed of gift
to son John. Wit: Mary BOUSH, Max BOUSH.

1DB364   7 Jul 1703:   Alice CORNICK and John
CORNICK deed of gift to daughter and granddaughter
Mary CORNICK and her sister Alif.   Wit: Francis
MORSE, William CAPPS.

1DB365   9 Jul 1703:   John HANDCOCK son of William to brother Simon a moiety of land which succee-
ded to me by the death of my brother William.   Wit:
C. COCKE, M. BOUSH.

1DB365   4 May 1703:   Richard WHITEHURST to son
John 50 acres.   Wit: Henry SNAYLE, Robert FOUNTAINE.

1DB366   8 Jul 1703:   William WHITE to Patrick
WHITE 100 acres in Knotts Island.   Wit: M. BOUSH,
Evan JONES, Jacob JOHNSON.

1DB369   10 Jan 1702/1 Sep 1703:   Jacob TAYLOR-
wife Rose; sons Jacob, John and William; daughters
Sarah, Elizabeth and Rose now wife of John MACLOUD.
ex: wife.   Wit: John FRIZELL, Mary PETREE, John
MACKIE.

1DB370   20 Dec 1702:   James HEATH - sons Thomas,
Robert and James; daughter Elizabeth EILAND; wife
Anne. Ex: wife.   Wit: Francis MORSE, William LURRY,
James DESMAN.

1DB374   27 Oct 1703/4 Nov 1703:   Thomas LAWSON
wife Rose, son Anthony (punchbowl which was grand-
gather Robert BRAY's), child wife goes with, son
George, daughters Frances and Anne.   Ex: wife.
Wit: Edward MOSELEY, Richard BOLTON, C. COCKE.

1DB378   19 Dec 1700/3 Feb 1703/4:   Thomas BENSON
sons William and Thomas, daughters Mary and Elizabeth.
Wit: John SMITH, Edward BAKER, William WARREN.

1DB378   1 Feb 1703/4:   Edward MOSELEY deed of
gift to children Hillary and Elizabeth.   Wit: John
FEREBEE, Robert FOUNTAINE.

1DB379   27 Nov 1703/5 Jan 1703/4:   Mathew PAL-
LETT - son John, daughter Mary, daughter Martha
COCKROFT and her son William.   Ex: son John.   Wit:
Thomas IVY, John MUNCREEF, John MURROUGH.

1DB382   2 Feb 1703/4:   Inventory of Jane TOOLY
by Francis JONES, William CATON, James TOOLY and
Richard SMITH sworn to by Mary TOOLY.

1DB382   3 Nov 1703:   Dennis CAPPS son of Henry
CAPPS sells land to John LEWIS.   Wit: C. COCKE,
Charles SAYES.

1DB384   1 Mar 1703:   Inventory of Thomas WALKE
by Richard CHURCH, Thomas COCKE, Thomas BUTT and
Thomas MASON of May 1695 - additional inventory
given by Edward MOSELEY.

1DB386   1 Mar 1703/4:   Appraisal of estate of
John HILL by Edward OLD and Cason MOORE sworn to by
Elizabeth HILL.

1DB389 3 May 1704: James MACOY heir at law
to Michael MACOY sells 150 acres to Robert BERRY
for 20 lbs. sterling. Wit: Thomas NILES, George
BECK, C. COCKE.

1DB390 11 May 1701/3 May 1704: Joseph DESHERN-
daughter Mary. Ex: daughter. Wit: John BROLUNE,
Peter WHASLEY, John CORNICK.

1DB389 ---1703/3 May 1704: Alexander KEELING -
eldest son Edward, wife Grace, sons Thorowgood,
Robert and William; daughters Grace, Anne and Elizabeth; granddaughter Pembrook. Ex: wife. Wit: John
THOMAS, John OKEHAM.

1DB391 24 April 1704: Richard JARVES of Coratuck power of attorney to Richard SANDERSON to re-
ceive legacies due him as marrying Dinah WOODHOUSE
daughter of John and Ruth WOODHOUSE.

1DB393 3 May 1704: Lewis PURVINE to brother
Joseph PURVINE 40 acres given him by my father Lewis
PURVINE's last will, part of a patent granted my
grandfather Thomas HALLE. Wit: George MASON, Sampson TREVETHAN, Thomas MASON.

1DB394 7 Jun 1704: Cason MORE to William MORE
134 acres called Long Ridge granted my grandfather
Edmund MORE and given Francis JONES who sold it to
my father Cason MORE. Wit: John MUNCREEF, Robert
BURROUGH, Joell CORNICK.

1DB397 29 May 1704: Rose LAWSON deed of gift
to children Anthony, Frances, George, Ann and Thomas.
Wit: C. COCKE, Richard CORBITT.

1DB398 7 Jun 1704: Joseph SANDERSON of Coratuck power of attorney to Joell CORNICK to repre-
sent him in suits brought by Edward OLD and Willoughby MERCHANT against him as having married Mary TOOLY
daughter of Thomas TOOLY and Admnx of her sister
Jane TOOLY, dec. Wit: Christopher BURROUGH, John
CARROWAY, Jr.

1DB400 ---/8 Jan 1704: Samuel WEBB - noncupative will - brother Anthony. Wit: Thomas TURNER,
Mary MALVAINE.

1DB404 6 Sep 1704: Henry WALSTONE deed of
gift to son Henry. Wit: John FULCHER, Charles SAYER.

1DB405 4 Nov 1704: Joan FULCHER deed of gift
to children George, Thomas, Frances and Ann LAWSON.
Wit: Charles SAYER, Richard CORBITT.

1DB406 4 Oct 1704: John CARROWAY deed of gift
to son John CARROWAY, Jr. 100 acres. Wit: John FERE-
BEE, Christopher BURROUGH.

1DB406 4 Oct 1704: Bartholomew WILLIAMSON deed
to brother John WILLIAMSON 100 acres. Wit: Christopher BURROUGH, John CARROWAY, Jr.

1DB407 4 Oct 1704: William DYER to Elizabeth
BASNETT 100 acres which her father John BASNETT
lived on - if she dies to male heirs of her mother
now wife of Owen SULLIVAN. Wit: Joel CORNICK, William MOSELEY.

1DB408 7 Sep 1703: William RUSSELL and William
BELL of NC to Thomas BODNAM for 30 lbs. 150 acres
given to William RUSSELL and his sister Ann now wife
of William BELL by William HILLYARD. Wit: John
RICHASON, John HELDON.

1DB410 4 Oct 1704: William WHITEHURST to brother Thomas WHITEHURST for 40 lbs. 150 acres - part
of a patent granted William GOLDSMITH. Wit: Thomas
KINGSTONE, David SCOTT, Jr., William GODFREY, John
WHITEHURST.

1DB416 2 May 1704: Richard SANDERSON of Corri-
tuck who married Grace daughter of John WOODHOUSE
power of attorney to Joel CORNICK. Wit: John RICHA-
SON, William MOSELEY.

1DB416 6 Sep 1704: John WOODHOUSE, Jr. and
wife, executor of Adam HAYES power of attorney to
Maximillian BOUSH to act in suit brought by Adam's
son Edward HAYES.

1DB416 3 Jan 1704/5: George KEMP and his wife,
one of daughters and legatees of Thomas SALLEY power
of attorney to Maximillian BOUSH to answer suit
brought by Richard CORBITT and Frances his wife,
Ex of Thomas SALLEY, dec.

1DB419 30 Sep 1704: Johan HANDCOCK wife of
Samuel HANDCOCK of Henrico Co. power of attorney to
brother Simon HANDCOCK. Wit: George MOSELEY, Ashall
HANDCOCK.

1DB419 17 Mar 1704/5: Solomon WHITE to Richard
SMITH for 70 lbs. 150 acres known as Rich Neck in
Blackwater precinct patented by Patrick WHITE father
of said Solomon. Wit: Thomas MASON.

1DB424 ---/1 Nov 1704: Jonas CHAPPELL - noncupative will - Mary WOODHOUSE daughter of Henry.
Wit: Solomon WHITE (38), Vesley HENLY (50).

1DB425 17 Jun 1705: Edward BONNEY and wife
Frances late widow of WALKER to Robert LAND deed of
gift of chattel. Wit: M. BOUSH, C. COCKE.

1DB427 14 Nov 1705: James and Sarah WHITE-
HURST to sons John and Thomas. Wit: Thomas WHITE-
HURST, John EDWARDS.

1DB427 4 Feb 1707/8: Jacob JOHNSON, Jr. deed
of gift to cousen Elizabeth WHICHARD daughter of
James and Mary WHICHARD. Wit: Christopher BURROUGH,
Robert BURROUGH.

1DB427 14 Nov 1705: James WHITEHURST and wife
Sarah deed of gift to son John of 75 acres - part of
land bought of cousen John JOHNSON. Wit: Thomas
WHITEHURST, John EDWARDS.

1DB430 7 Jun 1705: Edward BONNEY son of Richard, and wife Frances deed of gift of property given by Mrs. Ann BRAY to Frances, to Ann LAND now wife of Robert FOUNTAIN. Wit: M. BOUSH, C. COCKE.

1DB431 6 Sep 1705: Francis and Ann THOROW-GOOD to John and Anthony THOROWGOOD sons of brother John THOROWGOOD, dec. Wit: Thomas MASON, Henry SPRATT, Edward MOSELEY.

1DB432 8 Apr 1705/6 Sep 1705: Margery DICKSON - Timothy DENNIS, Otho RUSSELL. Ex: Otho RUSSELL. Wit: Mary PURVINE, Margaret BURNE, Richard BOLTON.

1DB433 19 May 1703/6 Jun 1705: Charles HENLEY - sons John and Thomas; grandchildren Charles and Sarah HENLEY; daughter Margaret; wife Useley. Ex: wife. Wit: Joseph LAND, Thomas COOPER.

1DB433 27 Apr 1705: Henry SOUTHERN deed of gift to sisters Elizabeth PHILPOTT and Jane MOORE. Wit: Rebecka OLD, Thomas CORPREW.

1DB433 3 Oct 1705: Rose LAWSON deed of gift to five children Anthony, George, Thomas, Frances and Anne, children of Thomas LAWSON, dec. Wit: Charles SAYER, Argall THOROWGOOD.

1DB436 7 Jun 1705: Richard CHURCH to grand-daughter Elizabeth THOROWGOOD daughter of Argall THOROWGOOD deed of gift of a mare in the care of Elizabeth's father-in-law Thomas TREVATHAN. Wit: Richard CORBITT, Robert BURROUGH.

1DB436 14 Mar 1704/3 Oct 1705: Sarah JACKSON - son Malbone SIMMONS, son Rudolphus MALBONE, daughter Ann HARRISON, daughter Elizabeth GODFREY, daughter Mary WICKER, grandson Godfrey MALBONE. Ex: son Peter MALBONE Wit: Thomas HEATH, James HEATH, Richard EILAND.

1DB438 3 Sep 1705: Richard CHURCH of Norfolk Co. power of attorney to son-in-law Richard CORBITT.

1DB439 19 Feb 1704/5/6 Jun 1705: Thomas ENG-LISH - son-in-law Roland SHAW, Rose COCKE, Elizabeth BROOKS, wife Mary. Ex: wife. Wit: Mark POWELL, John JAMES, Ann BRIDGER.

1DB440 7 Aug 1704: Jehue COCKROFT discharges father-in-law Mark POWELL of everything given by my mother. Wit: Nathaniel MCCLANEHAN, Jehue COCKROFT.

1DB441 6 Dec 1705: James KEMP, Sr. deed of gift to granddaughter Ann daughter of son George KEMP and Mary his wife. Wit: John THRUSTON, Richard CORBITT.

1DB443 24 Aug 1705/5 Oct 1705: Robert PEALE - sons Thomas and Henry, wife Rose. Ex: wife. Wit: Wit: Sampson TREVATHAN, Charles SAYER.

1DB445 27 Oct 1705: William MOORE - sons James and William, daughter Elizabeth, wife. Ex: wife. Wit: Edward ATTWOOD, Cason MOORE.

1DB446 3 Jan 1705/6: Owen and Ruth SULLIVAN to brother Morris SULLIVAN 120 acres given me by my father John SULLIVAN. Wit: Timothy DORNE, Thomas FRANKLIN.

1DB448 6 Feb 1705/6: William SHIPP to brother Lancaster SHIPP 100 acres. Wit: Alexander HARVEY, Otho RUSSELL.

1DB450 6 Feb 1705/6: Amy WOODHOUSE widow of Capt. Henry deed of gift to son Henry, daughters Sarah, Isabella, Amy and Mary. Wit: Thomas SPRATT, James COTTEN, Peter YEATES, James HAYNES.

1DB452 4 Dec 1700/6 Mar 1705/6: Benoni BUR-ROUGHS - eldest son Christopher (Dam Neck), sons Robert and Benjamin, three daughters Mary, Barbary and Elizabeth, wife Mary. Ex: wife. Wit: Mark POWELL, Henry LINTON, George SMITH.

1DB455 3 Jul 1706: John SIMMONS of Surry Co., Va. and Mary his wife daughter of Thomas COCKE, dec. to Lt. Thomas SCOTT, Sr. for 100 lbs. 125 and 62½ acres in Princess Anne Co. Wit: Joel CORNICK, John BOLITHOE, William MOSELEY.

1DB462 3 Jul 1706: George SMITH deed to son Tully. Wit: William SMITH, Richard CORBITT, Lancaster SHIPP.

1DB464 5 Aug 1706/4 Nov 1706: Thomas SCOTT - eldest son David, son Thomas, daughter Margaret, wife Frances. Ex: wife, David and Margaret. Wit: David SCOTT, Richard BALL, Richard CORBITT.

1DB464 ---/18 May 1706: James LAMOUNT - grandsons James, Edward, John and Thomas LAMOUNT, granddaughter Mary MACKIE daughter of John MACKIE, wife Sarah, son Edward. Ex: wife and son Edward. Wit: Robert BELL, William HUNTER, John RICHASON.

1DB465 2 Mar 1704/5/1 Oct 1707: Thomas COCK-ROFT - brother James HARPER, sister Sarah and Ann POWELL, brother John COCKROFT. Wit: Mark POWELL, Edward BRUSHBANK.

1DB466 4 Mar 1706/7: Alice CORNICK widow of William CORNICK to son-in-law John CORNICK and his daughter Mary, son Lemuell IVY, dec. Wit: William CAPPS, Joell CORNICK, James DAUGEMENT

1DB467 13 Apr 1706/3 Jul 1707: John BIBBERY - John THOROWGOOD son of LtCol. Adam THOROWGOOD, Francis eldest son of Adam THOROWGOOD. Ex: Adam THOROW-GOOD. Wit: Argall THOROWGOOD, William WEBSTER.

1DB467 1 Dec 1705/1 May 1706: Mary LOVITT - sons Lancaster, Thomas, Adam, John and William; daughter Elizabeth KEELING wife of Thomas and their children Mary and Thomas; William's son William and daughter Mary; granddaughter Ann KEMP; daughter Sarah RICHASON wife of Thomas. Ex: son William. Overseers: Col. Adam THOROWGOOD, John CARROWAY, Jr.,

and Robert FOUNTAIN. Wit: Robert CARTWRIGHT, Katherine CARTWRIGHT, M. BOUSH.

1DB469   20 Jan 1702/4 Sep 1706:   William WALS-
WORTH - son William, wife Frances, John FRIZELL,
Daniel FRIZELL. Ex: wife. Wit: John MACKIE, John
HUSON.

1DB469   27 Jul 1705/6 Mar 1706/7:   Henry HARRI-
SON - daughter Mary, wife Frances. Ex: wife. Wit:
Edward ATTWOOD, James LAMOUNT, Edward LAMOUNT.

1DB469   13 Nov 1706/6 Mar 1706/7:   William
SALMON - brother Charles EDWARDS, son William, daugh-
ter Elizabeth, wife Mary. Ex: wife. Wit: Anthony
WEBB, Richard STONE.

1DB469   30 Dec 1704/6 Dec 1705:   John BRITTOON
- Richard SMITH, daughter-in-law Ann ASHBY. Ex:
Richard SMITH. Wit: John ASHBY, John WILLIAMS.

1DB470   23 Sep 1705/1 May 1706:   John GODFREY,
Jr. - son Jonathan (manor plantation, son Arthur
(Evens Neck), son John, daughter Dinah, wife Eliza-
beth, child wife goes with. Ex: wife. Wit: Thomas
BUTT, John EDWARDS, John MURPHEY, Elizabeth GODFREY.

1DB470   30 Jan 1695/6/2 Apr 1707:   Mary RAVENS
- grandsons Hugh, John, Henry and Robert WHITEHURST,
granddaughters Mary and Elizabeth WHITEHURST, grandson Henry SMITH, grandson Henry NICHOLAS, his aunt
Mary wife of Richard SMITH, grandsons Edward and
William TRANTER, John EDMONDS, daughters Ellener
and Mary SMITH wife of Richard. Ex: daughter Mary.
Wit: Joseph EDWARDS, Steven PEW, John SMITH, John
BARRINGTON.

1DB471   15 Nov 1707:   James MACOY son of Mackael
MACOY, dec. to John BOLITHOE for 5 shillings 215
acres and 115 acres. Wit: David SCOTT, Jr., Sampson TREVETHAN, George MOSELEY.

1DB473   2 Sep 1707:   William MILLER and wife
Mary, only daughter of Robert HODGE, dec. to George
MASON for 5 shillings 280 acres. Wit: William MOSE-
LEY, Alexander HARVEY.

1DB476   1 Dec 1707:   David SCOTT, Jr. son and
heir of Thomas SCOTT to John HOPKINS for 10 lbs.
100 acres. Wit: Robert BELL, Thomas SCOTT, C. COCKE.

1DB481   30 Dec 1706/5 Nov 1707:   James KEMP -
eldest son George, son James, son-in-law Thomas
WISHARD and Mary his wife, wife Ann. Ex: wife and
son George. Wit: John THRUSTON, Ben ROBERTS, Richard
CORBITT.

1DB481   6 Sep 1703/2 Oct 1706:   John OAKHAM -
son-in-law Richard LESTER, his brother John, wife
Isabell, son William. Ex: wife. Wit: James DAUGE,
John BONNEY, William CATHRILL.

1DB482 6 Nov 1707: Edward MOSELEY deed of gift to children Hillary and Elizabeth. Wit: Christopher BURROUGH, Argall THOROWGOOD.

1DB491 8 Apr 1708: Katherine HALL deed of gift to daughter Martha HALL daughter of Thomas, Mary LAND, son Francis LAND, son Job GASKINS. Wit: M. BOUSH, Solomon JONES, Conner CALLAHAN.

1DB493 2 Oct 1706: Eliner BIGGS to children Jaber and Eliner children of John BIGGS deed of gift - three daughters Elizabeth KENTON wife of John, Jane SMITH wife of John SMITH and Eliner LEWIS, wife of Thomas. Wit: JONES, C. COCKE.

1DB495 8 Aug 1707/3 Sep 1707: George SMITH - sons William, Tully, George, John and Benony; grandchildren Charles and Margaret SMITH. Ex: son William. Wit: John SHURLEY, Richard CORBITT, Tully EMPEROR.

1DB497 5 Mar 1706/7: Michall JONES deed of gift to daughter Mary SIMMONS wife of Malbone SIMMONS 50 acres in Knotts Island. Wit: Thomas SPRATT, Joel CORNICK, Reodolphus MALBONE.

1DB502 7 May 1707: Margaret THOROWGOOD deed of gift to children John, Anthony, Margret and Mary children of Col. John THOROWGOOD, dec. Wit: Elizabeth THOROWGOOD, William MOSELEY.

1DB503 21 Sep 1706: Mathew MATHIAS late of Princess Anne Co. and son and heir of Mathew MATHIAS, Sr. to John EDMONDS for 2600 lbs. of pork 40 acres. Wit: Thomas WHITEHURST, William SMYTH.

1DB506 11 Oct 1707: Edward WOOD and wife Catherine deed of gift to sons Edward and Mark. Wit: Bartholomew WILLIAMSON, Richard WILLIAMSON.

1DB509 2 Jun 1708: William SMITH deed to brother Tully for 50 lbs. land George SMITH died on. Wit: Charles SAYER, Christopher BURROUGH.

1DB510 2 Jun 1708: John CARROWAY, Sr. to son John CARROWAY, Jr. 150 acres. Wit: John MOSELEY, Richard CORBITT.

1DB511 21 Aug 1706: Peter GRINTO son of William GRINTO power of attorney to Richard CORBITT to recover legacy from uncle John GRINTO.

1DB511 24 Mar 1707/8/2 Jun 1708: Thomas ILIFFE - wife and four daughters. Ex: son-in-law Aron FENTRESS. Trustees: John PALLETT and Robert BURROUGH. Wit: Richard SMITH, Phillis BURGESS, Mark POWELL.

1DB513 7 Apr 1708: Edward and Susanna LAMOUNT to Lewis CONNER for 1000 lbs. sterling 1775 acres of marsh sold to James LAMOUNT and given to son Edward in his will. Wit: Henry JENKINS, John FULCHER, Henry CHAPMAN.

1DB516 7 Apr 1708: John SOLLY son and heir of Thomas SOLLY to Richard CORBITT for 60 lbs. 200 acres South side of Eastern Branch. Wit: Edward MOSELEY, Adam THOROWGOOD, Christopher COCKE, Jacob JOHNSON.

1DB518   Sep 1706:   About 1697 William GRINTO, dec. had us brand horses for each of his three children he had by late wife Mary - John, Grace and William.   Thomas ETHERINGTON, John MALALAHAN.

1DB522   7 Oct 1708:   John MOY, Sr. to son Richard MOY deed of gift of 100 acres adjoining Bear Quarter. Wit: C. COCKE, George HANCOCK, Henry SPRATT.

1DB253   7 Jan 1707/8/2 Sep 1708:   William LOVITT - son William, daughters Mary and Ann, wife Ann. Entrust brother John and friend Joseph DOLLAR to take care of son (under 14).   Wit: Joseph DOLLAR, Sarah MORRIS, Mark POWELL.

1DB526   4 Sep 1708:   Edward MOSELEY only surviving purchaser of 51 acres - William MOSELEY, dec. one of purchasers desired sons William and Richard to have choice.   Wit: John FEREBEE, Anthony WALKE.

1DB528   2 Jan 1708:   Morris SULLIVEN to Joseph LANE for 6 lbs. 20 acres known as Cow Pen Ridge, part of patent granted Owen SULLIVAN 7 Nov 1700. Wit: John PALLETT, Richard CORBITT, Thomas HARRISON.

DEED BOOK TWO

2DB14   21 Jan 1706:   Richard BONNEY - sons
John, Richard, William and Edward; daughters Sarah
FRANKLIN, Mary DAUGE, Constance CURLON, Phebe LAND,
Margaret MCCLALLAN and Dinah; wife.   Ex: son John.
Wit: John JAMES, Edward JAMES.
     2DB18   8 Sep 1709:   William ROYLY deed of gift
to son Thomas ROYLY.   Wit: Peter MALBONE, Robert
BURROUGH.
     2DB19   9 Sep 1709:   Charles SAYER deed of gift
to son-in-law John THOROWGOOD son of Col. John THO-
ROWGOOD, and his brother Anthony.   Wit: Sampson
TREVETHAN, Thomas WALKE.
     2DB20   3 Oct 1707/5 Jun 1709:   Alice THROWER -
cousen Walter JONES and his wife Elizabeth, cousen
Sarah LOWRY, cousen Alice JONES, cousen Betty JONES,
cousen Lilyam JONES, cousen John CORNICK, cousen
Sarah HANSOM.   Ex: Walter JONES.   Wit: Thomas CRISPE,
Walter JONES.
     2DB20   17 Sep 1708/6 Jul 1709:   Alice CORNICK -
sons Anthony and Thomas IVY, daughter Aliff CORNICK,
grandson Morris FITZGERALD, granddaughter Elizabeth
ANGUS.   Ex: son Thomas.   Wit: Richard CORBITT, Henry
LINTON, Patrick ANGUS.
     2DB25   2 Apr 1709:   William MOSELEY son of Wil-
liam and Blandina MOSELEY to Richard MOSELEY land
which belonged to my grandfather Richard POOLE.   Wit:
Edward MOSELEY, Robert BURROUGH, George POOLE.
     2DB36   27 May 1710/5 Jul 1710:   Jacob JOHNSON -
grandsons William and Jacob sons of Jacob JOHNSON,
grandson John WISHARD son of James WISHARD, grand-
daughter Mary WISHARD daughter of James and Mary
WISHARD, granddaughter Jacomin WISHARD, granddaughter
Elizabeth WISHARD, son-in-law James WISHARD, son
Jacob JOHNSON, wife Ann.   Ex: son Jacob.   Wit:
Charles ___, John KEMP, C. COCKE.
     2DB38   12 Apr 1710/1 Nov 1710:   Jacob JOHNSON,
Jr. - sons William and Jacob, daughters Mary and
Jacomin.   Ex: wife and James LANGLEY.   Wit: William
WISHART, Mary MILLIGAN, Jeremiah LANGLEY.

2DB43   1 Dec 1710/6 Dec 1710:   Johanna COLLINS -
Daniel MACLOUD, Sarah HOLMES daughter of John HOP-
KINS, daughter Elizabeth COLLINS, son Francis COL-
LINS.   Ex: Cousin John JAMISON.   Wit: Hatha JONES,
C. COCKE.

2DB52   3 May 1710:   Mark POWELL deed of gift
to daughter Ann - if she dies without heirs to daughter Sarah.   Wit: George MOSELEY, Owen MATHIS.

2DB54   21 Feb 1719/- May 1710:   Edward LAMOUNT -
sons James (Hickory Neck), Thomas, John, Edward and
Henry; wife Susanna.   Ex: wife.   Wit: John CORNICK,
John BROWN, William TAYLOR, Jacob TAYLOR.

2DB66   23 Oct 1710/3 Jan 1710:   William SMYTH -
wife Ann; three daughters Margret, Elizabeth and
Mary.   Ex: wife.   Wit: C. COCKE, Tully SMYTH.

2DB70   5 Oct 1709:   James HAYNES deed of gift
to son John.   Wit: William HUNTER, John WEBLIN.

2DB70   20 Jan 1710/5 Mar 1710:   Owen MATHIS -
mother-in-law Ann CARLEY, daughter Mary, wife Amy.
Ex: wife.   Wit: Malachy HARFORD, John LESTER, William
MUNCREEF.

2DB73   5 Oct 1709:   Anthony RICHMOND to brother
Robert RICHMOND for 15 lbs. 50 acres.   Wit: John
PALLETT, Thomas PHILLIPS, Robert BOND.

2DB73   6 Apr 1709:   Robert MURDEN son of Robert
MURDEN to John MURDEN for 8 lbs. 100 acres.   Wit:
Richard CORBITT, George HANCOCK, William SMYTH,
Sampson TREVETHAN.

2DB75   6 Apr 1709:   Robert MURDEN son and lega-
tee of John MURDEN late of Norfolk Co. to John MURDEN
for 8 lbs. 100 acres on South Branch of Elizabeth River
beginning at Richard BUTT's line.   Wit: Richard CORBITT,
George HANCOCK, William SMYTH, Sampson TREVETHAN.

2DB77   6 Sep 1710:   Edward LAND deed of gift to
children Jonathan, Edward, Hillary, Mary and Elizabeth.   Wit: Robert LAND, Daniel FRIZZELL.

2DB88   24 Sep 1710/1 Nov 1710:   Alexander LIL-
BURN - sons William and Lemuel; daughters Amy, Jane
and Elizabeth; wife.   Ex: William.   Wit: C. COCKE,
Henry CHAPMAN.

2DB90   20 Feb 1710/4 Sep 1711:   Nathaniel MC-
CLENAHAN - brother David; sons Andrew, David and
John; daughter Ann; wife; Josias MACKIE, Christopher
COCKE.   Ex: wife.   Wit: Ann HANCOCK, Tully SMYTH,
Dugal BLAW.

2DB97   16 Apr 1711:   James WILLIAMSON - son
Charles, wife Elenor.   Ex: brother Charles.   Wit:
William THOMAS, William WEST, William BROWN.

2DB102   4 Jan 1711:   John WOODHOUSE, Jr. to
brother Henry now of NC 133 acres.   Wit: Sarah RICH-
ASON, John RICHASON, Thomas FINCKLEY, James HAYNES,
Thomas PHILLIPS.

2DB109   10 Jul 1712:   Robert FOUNTAIN deed of
gift to son Roger, daughters Mary and Frances. Wit:
C. COCKE, Lewis PURVINE.

2DB122   1 Sep 1710:   Joel CORNICK to John CORNICK
land given him by William CORNICK, dec. Wit: F. MORSE,
Edward CANNON, William CAPPS.

2DB140   4 May 1710:   William NICKOLS to son-in-
law Bryan CULLEN, his daughter Mary. Wit: C. COCKE.

2DB147   3 Jul 1710:   Jane BROOK deed of gift
to children William and Sarah. Wit: John SMITH,
Samuell SICKLEMORE.

2DB148   20 Apr 1710:   Richard CARROWAY - brother
Thomas land given me by my father John; brothers Wil-
liam and James; sister Elizabeth; cousen Elizabeth
WHITEHURST. Ex: father. Wit: Charles WILLIAMSON,
Richard CORBITT, John WEBLIN.

2DB149   31 Dec 1709:   Richard SMITH - sons John
and Richard, daughter Mary wife of John POTT, wife
Sarah, son-in-law William ASHBY. Ex: wife. Wit:
Joell CORNICK, John CORNICK, William CAPPS.

2DB149   18 Mar 1706/7:   Josiah HANNAY - Capt.
Horatio WOODHOUSE. Ex: Capt. Horatio WOODHOUSE.
Wit: Francis SPANN, Sr., Francis SPANN, Jr., Ann
SPANN.

2DB150   ---/5 Apr 1709:   Edward ATTWOOD - sons
Thomas, William and John; John's sons Edward and
Francis; Mary daughter of my son John WOODHOUSE;
daughters Frances MOORE and her daughter Mary HAR-
RISON; daughter Amy, sister Elizabeth. Ex: son
Thomas. Wit: William RUTLAND, Thomas HARRISON.

2DB150   ---/27 Nov 1709:   James PETERS - cousen
James LOWRY son of James LOWRY, cousen James HANCOCK
son of George and Mary HANCOCK, cousen Capt. George
HANCOCK. Ex: Capt. George HANCOCK. Wit: C. COCKE,
John JAMISON.

2DB152   ---/26 Apr 1711:   James MOORE - brother
William, sister Elizabeth, cousen Cason MOORE. Ex:
Cason MOORE. Wit: James HAYNES, Ruth SULLIVAN, Thomas
PHILLIPS.

2DB152   ---/8 Jan 1710/11:   Samuel WHITEHURST -
brothers John, Thomas, Richard and William; mother
Sarah; sisters Sarah, Anne and Elizabeth; father
James. Ex: father. Wit: John CARROWAY, Sr., Stephen
PEW.

2DB152   ---/29 Jan 1709/10:   William CATEN -
sons John, Solomon, Moses, William and Thomas; wife
Jane; daughter Elizabeth and three other daughters.
Ex: wife. Wit: Thomas CORPREW, John WARD, John
OLIVER.

2DB194   2 Mar 1713:   Solomon JONES deed of gift
to wife's children Edward, John, Thomas and Henry
LAMOUNT. Wit: Samuel SHEPHERD, Thomas HARRISON.

2DB196   24 Apr 1707/5 Jul 1714:   Robert FOUNTAIN -
wife Ann: son Roger; daughters Frances and Mary, Col.
Edward MOSELEY.   Ex: wife and Horatio WOODHOUSE.   Wit:
Francis LAND, Robert LAND, Richard DOUDE, John SNAILE.

2DB220   4 Jun 1714:   Peter GRINTO to John GRINTO
plantation heired from father William GRINTO.   Wit:
Richard CORBITT, William CAPPS, M. BOUSH.

2DB227   7 Jun 1714:   William SMITH to William
SMITH, Jr. 60 acres.   Wit: Argall THOROWGOOD, John
COCKROFT, Samuell SHEPHERD.

2DB229   4 Aug 1714:   John SHIRLEY deed of gift
to children John and George.   Wit: Christopher BUR-
ROUGH, Hillary MOSELEY, Anthony LAWSON.

2DB233   22 Apr 1711/4 Mar 1712:   Joseph GOODACRE
- brother Thomas, godson Philip HUGINS, William GOOD-
ACRE, wife Sarah.   Ex: wife.   Wit: James HARPER, James
LAMOUNT.

2DB244   29 May 1712:   Division of goods and chattel
of Thomas IVY - wife Ursula and four youngest children
Anthony, Lemuell, George and Sarah.   Wit: Charles WIL-
LIAMSON, John CARROWAY, Sr.

DEED BOOK THREE

3DB5   1 Feb 1710/6 Apr 1714:   Michaell FENTRISS,
Sr. - sons John, James, Michaell, William, Moses and
Aaron; daughter Rebecca wife of Henry WHITEHURST,
daughter Mary wife of Thomas WITES, grandson Francis
SHIPP; daughter Elizabeth; wife Ann. Ex: wife and
James. Wit: M. BOUSH, Thomas EWELL, Richard COCKIN.
    3DB7   17 Aug 1713/5 Apr 1714:   Elenor WILLE -
daughters Mary, Ann, Elinor, Sarah and Elizabeth;
sons Owen and Richard. Ex: Owen. Wit: William
SHIP, John RATHEY.
    3DB8   20 Aug 1714/4 Oct 1714:   John RICHASON -
daughter Ann MORSE wife of Francis; son Thomas; his
son John; grandsons John JACKSON and Richason MORSE.
Ex: son Thomas. Wit: Horatio WOODHOUSE, Peter WAPLES,
Richard CROMPTON.
    3DB9   2 May 1714/1 Nov 1714:   Ashall HANCOCK -
brother William, sisters Mary, Elizabeth and Dinah,
cosing James HANCOCK, cosen Elizabeth HANCOCK, brother George, James WISHARD. Ex: brother William.
Wit: Henry COLLINS, Charles GRIFFIN, John JAMASON.
    3DB12   26 Sep 1713/5 Apr 1714:   Charles GIBSON
of Blackwater - wife Elenor, children. Ex: wife.
Wit: Elener BIGG, Jr., John OLIVER.
    3DB17   28 Oct 1714/6 Dec 1714:   John GISBORNE -
sons John, Edward and William; daughters Susanna and
Mary; wife Jane. Ex: wife. Wit: Richard CAPPS, John
DAULLY, Andrew PEACOCK.
    3DB26   5 Mar 1714:   James WHITEHURST elder to
John son of John WHITEHURST, dec. for 2 lbs. 100
acres. Wit: Richard CORBETT, Lewis BACKER, Richard
NICKOLES.
    3DB33   3 Mar 1714:   James WHITEHURST to son John
deed of gift of 75 acres near Three Runs. Wit: Rich-
are CORBETT, John WHITEHURST, Nathaniel NICKLES.
    3DB33   3 Mar 1714:   James WHITEHURST to son Tho-
mas 100 acres near Three Runs. Wit: Richard CORBETT,
John WHITEHURST, Nathaniel NICKLES.
    3DB33   3 Mar 1714:   James WHITEHURST to son James
100 acres on South side Eastern Branch. Wit: Thomas
WHITEHURST, Henry WHITEHURST.

3DB36   31 May 1715:   Josiah MORRIS to brother William MORRIS for 5 shillings 150 acres called Ye Old Plantacon on South side of Nannys Creek on Wolf Pit Point.   Wit: C. COCKE, G. HALLIDAY.

3DB44   5 Jul 1715:   John WOODHOUSE TO Thomas ATTWOOD for 5 shillings 48 acres which Lewis PURVINE sold to John FULCHER, Jr. who died intestate and WOODHOUSE is uncle and heir of FULCHER.   Wit: John LOVETT, Lewis PURVINE, Richard CROMPTON.

3DB52   27 Apr 1715:   Anthony RICHMOND to Robert RICHMOND for 4000 lbs. pork 60 acres formerly land of father Robert.   Wit: William BENSON, Owen MAGRAVY, Richard CROMPTON.

3DB54   1 Apr 1715:   William RICHMOND to brother Anthony RICHMOND 60 acres.   Wit: Richard CROMPTON, John LOVETT, Peter HUTCHASON.

3DB64   1 Feb 1714:   Adam KEELING to Adam, John and William KEELING sons of Thomas KEELING, dec. for 5 shillings 150 acres.   Wit: M. BOUSH, Richard CROMPTON, Charles WILLIAMSON.

3DB69   2 Feb 1714:   Adam KEELING to Thomas KEELING eldest son of Thomas, dec. for 4 lbs 10 shillings 100 acres.   Wit: M. BOUSH, Richard CROMPTON, Charles WILLIAMSON.

3DB72   1 Oct 1715:   Sarah BONNEY wife of John BONNEY power of attorney to brother William BONNEY to relinquish dower right on plantation where my my mother Mary HUTCHINSON now liveth.   Wit: John WATTSON, Andrew PEACOCK.

3DB73   7 Dec 1715:   David and Sarah LEGAT to William WICKER for 25 lbs. 100 acres bequeathed me by my dec. father John LEGAT, confirmed by my brother John LEGAT.

3DB81   3 Jan 1715:   Thomas BEESLEY to John CORNICK for 5 lbs. 150 acres inherited from father Thomas.   Wit: Joel CORNICK, John JARVES, Edward JAMES.

3DB85   3 May 1715:   Samuel SPRUILL of Chowan precinct NC and wife Elizabeth daughter of Stephen SWAINE to Thomas SHEPHERD for 52 lbs. 454 acres on Knotts Island which Solomon WHITE gave his sister Elizabeth who married SWAINE.   Wit: Joel CORNICK, Alef CORNICK, Honour COX.

3DB86   28 Aug 1715:   William and Mary FENTRISS to Thomas STANDLY for 5 lbs. 4 shillings 25 acres which belonged to David MURROW elder which he gave to son Alexander who left it to daughter Mary who married FENTRIS.   Wit: George WILLIAMSON, Richard STANDLEY, Eavem STANLEY.

3DB87   6 Sep 1715:   Thomas and Elizabeth SCOTT to John HOPKINS for 40 lbs. half of tract of 142 acres which he inherited from father Thomas.   Wit: George BOUSH, John MURDIN, David SCOTT, Jr., Lemuel NEWTON.

3DB90   31 Jul 1716: John CARROWAY, Sr. and
wife Ann deed of gift of 100 acres each to sons
Thomas, William and James at Bowin's River. Wit:
Richard CORBET, Mary CANON.

3DB106   16 Aug 1716: Mark POWELL and wife Ann
to daughter Ann deed to land called Ye Ferry. Wit:
George MOSELEY, Christopher BURROUGH.

eDB110   1 Oct 1716: William OAKHAM to Denis
CAPPS for 18 lbs. 100 acres inherited from father
John. Wit: Thomas ALLBRITON, William CAPPS.

3DB112   4 Mar 1716: Ruth SHEPHERD power of
attorney to Patrick JONES to acknowledge release
of dower right to land husband Thomas is selling.
Wit: Cornelius JONES, Timothy IVES.

3DB115   6 Nov 1714/4 Apr 1716: William GRIFFEN
- daughter Mary, wife Sarah. Ex: wife. Wit: Lemuel
HOLMES, Henry CHAPMAN.

3DB116   4 Dec 1714/3 Jan 1714: Thomas KEELING
- sons Thomas, Adam, John and William; daughters
Margaret, Elizabeth, Mary and Amy; mother Mary LOVET,
wife Elizabeth. Ex: wife. Wit: James HAYNES, John
LOVET, William FLEAR.

3DB116   8 Jun 1717/4 Arp 1715: William MARTIN -
son Henry, grandson William, granddaughters Ann and
Rebeckah. Ex: son Henry. Wit: William LILBURN,
Martha LILBURN, John FORGERSON, Elizabeth FORGIES.

3DB117   30 Mar 1715/4 May 1715: John WOODHOUSE,
Sr. - son Horatio, daughter Mary. Ex: brother Hora-
tio. Wit: George CLARKE, Thomas BRINSON, George
HALLIDAY.

3DB117   9 May 1713/6 Jun 1716: David SCOTT,
Sr. - cousen Thomas SCOTT son of brother, cousen
Margaret, cousen David SCOTT, Jr. son of brother
Thomas. Ex: David, Jr. Wit: Robert BELL, Sarah
BELL.

3DB118   13 Mar 1712/1 Aug 1716: Frances FOWLER
oldest daughter of George, dec. - sister-in-law
Argent COCKE, sister Ann COCKE, sister-in-law Mary
and Elizabeth COCKE, sister Mrs. Pembrook FOWLER,
father-in-law Christopher COCKE. Ex: Pembrook.
Wit: William HUNTER, C. COCKE, M. BOUSH, Elizabeth
LENARD

3DB118   14 Jul 1716/1 Aug 1716: Ann JOHNSON -
son Randolph LOVIT, sons George and James KEMP, son-
in-law Thomas WISHARD. Ex: Thomas WISHARD. Wit:
C. COCKE, William WISHARD.

3DB130   2 Mar 1715/16: George BULLOCK deed of
gift to granddaughter Mary SIMMONS wife of Malbone
SIMMONS 20 acres. Wit: Michell JONES, Sr. Michell
JONES.

3DB132   6 Nov 1716: Edward WOOD, Sr. deed of
gift to son William. Wit: Ann NASH, Thomas NASH, Sr.

3DB133   1 Oct 1716:   William WALSTONE to John
STYRING for 5 shillings 56 acres, part of a tract
which was formerly land of Thomas WALSTON, grandfather of said William.   Wit: Joseph WHITE, Elizabeth WHITE, Richard CROMPTON.

3DB136   3 Jun 1716:   Evan JONES deed of gift to
son Patrick 200 acres.   Wit: Edward MOSELEY.

3DB137   2 Jan 1716:   William and Frances WEST
deed of gift of 80 acres to brother-in-law William
BROWN.   Wit: Richard STONE, George MOSELEY.

3DB138   5 Feb 1716/17:   John and Sarah CARRU-
THERS and brother William and wife Elizabeth for
15 lbs. 155 acres to John DAULEY, part of patent
taken by Denis DAULEY and given to daughter Elizabeth.   Wit: John GISBORN, Edward CANNON.

3DB140   10 Nov 1716/2 Jan 1716:   Ann SEALEY -
daughter Elizabeth, grandson William DOBS, daughter
Mary, son John.   Ex: John.   Wit: Solomon KEATON,
Moses KEATON, Andrew PEACOCK.

3DB140   1 Oct 1716/5 Dec 1716:   James WHITE -
William DENNEY son of Katherine DENNEY, Thomas DE-
VAUGHAN.   Ex: Thomas WISHARD.   Wit: Robert HUMPHREY,
Thomas TOMLINSON, Arthur BLAKE.

1DB140   14 Aug 1716/5 Dec 1716:   Samuel SICKLE-
MORE - wife Sarah, children, Mary BRINDLE wife of
Lawrence BRINDLE.   Wit: David SPANN, William DYER.

3DB141   26 Jul 1714/5 Dec 1716:   Thomas BROCK -
sons Thomas, James, Samuel and John; daughters Mary
WEBLIN and Mary BROOKS, grandchildren Henry and
Hester FITZGERALD; wifeElizabeth.   Ex: wife.   Wit:
Sarah SYMMONS, William CAPPS, Henry SIMMONS.

3DB141   2 Oct 1716/2 Jan 1716:   Richard HOSKINS -
sister Mary BROCK, Margret and Mary daughters of
James and Mary BROCK.   Ex: James and Mary.   Wit:
Adam BROUGHTON, Thomas HARVEY, Sr., Argall THOROW-
GOOD.

3DB141   5 Nov 1716/5 Dec 1716:   Christopher
COCKE - daughters Mary, Elizabeth, Ann and Argent;
John BOLITHOE, Maximillian BOUSH; tuition of Mary,
Ann and Argent unto uncle and ant BOLITHOE, tuition
of Elizabeth to uncle William COCKE; Ann FURLONG;
Sampson TREVETHAN.   Ex: Capt. Henry CHAPMAN, John
BOLITHOE and Max BOUSH.   Wit: Thomas WISHARD, Mary
BOLITHOE.

3DB143   2 May 1715/7 Mar 1716:   Francis MORSE -
sons Baron, Francis, Thomas and John; daughter Elizabeth; wife.   Ex: wife.   Overseers: John CORNICK,
Horatio WOODHOUSE.   Wit: Thomas HEATH, James HEATH,
Thomas BROWN.

3DB157   21 May 1717:   Appraisement of estate of
George POOLE, Jr. by Thomas LAND, John SNAILE, John
PALLETT, and P. COWELL sworn to by relict Sarah.

3DB157 11 Mar 1717/5 Jun 1717: Alexander
MCCLENAHAN - wife, after her death to George SIM-
MONS son of Henry and Mary SIMMONS. Ex: wife.
Wit: John MOY, Henry SIMMONS, Thomas CATTEN.

3DB158 18 Dec 1716/1 May 1717: Thomas OWENS
- sons John and Thomas, daughters Rose and Lucy,
wife Elizabeth. Ex: wife. Wit: Samuell SHEPHERD,
James DOLLAR, Thomas GOODAKER.

3DB158 16 Apr 1717/5 Jun 1717: Benjamin
MOSELEY - wife Elizabeth, sons Daniel, Benjamin
and Axwell, daughter Dinah. Ex: wife. Wit: Edward MOSELEY, William BROCK.

3DB160 3 Apr 1717: Reodolphus MALBONE deed
of gift to wife Elizabeth. Wit: Richard CROMPTON,
Malbone SIMMONS, Thomas EVTNSON.

3DB160 3 Apr 1717: Edmond PORTER son and
heir of John PORTER power of attorney to Anthony
WALKE or John ACKISS. Wit: John ACKISS, Katherine
SIMMONS, William HANCOCK, Ann KEMPE.

3DB162 3 Dec 1716: William FENTRIS and wife
Mary to John SCOTT 80 acres FENTRIS had in right
of his wife Mary left her by Alexander MURRAY.
Wit: James NICKOLLS, George KEMPE, Richard CORBITT.

3DB165 10 Feb 1714: Ann and James FENTRIS exrs
of Michaell FENTRIS discharge to each other. Wit:
Tully SMYTH, Ann SMYTH.

3DB166 1 Oct 1717: Lawrence DAWLEY to Alex-
ander LEGGET for 5 lbs. 50 acres formerly held by
Lawrence DAWLEY father of said Lawrence. Wit: Henry
WHITE, Richard CROMPTON, Lewis PURVINE.

3DB169 2 Oct 1717: John CARROWAY, Sr. deed of
gift to son-in-law John WHITEHURST and daughter Ann
his wife. Wit: Tully SMYTH, John MARTINDALE.

3DB169 10 Sep 1717/6 Nov 1717: William WICKER
- son Richard; daughters Mary, Sarah, Hannah and
Betty. Wit: Solomon WHITE, Malbone SIMMONS, Richard JONES.

3DB174 12 Oct 1717: Inventory of James ANGUS
by Charles SAYER, Tully SMYTH and George SMYTH.

3DB175 14 May 1717/4 Dec 1717: Thomas KEATON
- brother William, sister Sarah, brothers James and
Moses. Ex: brother Moses. Wit: Benjamin COMINS,
John SEALEY, Solomon KEATON, John SMITH.

3DB177 13 Mar 1716/3 Jul 1717: Peter CRASHLEY -
granddaughter Sarah EATON daughter of Michael EATON,
daughter Ann wife of Michael EATON. Wit: William
DYER, John EATON.

3DB184 5 Sep 1717/5 Feb 1717: James WISHARD -
wife Mary, children Francis and Dinah, son John,
son Jacob JOHNSON WISHARD, duaghter Elizabeth - seven
children. Ex: wife, Thomas WISHARD and George HAN-
COCK. Wit: William HANCOCK, Rose PARTREE.

3DB185   18 Dec 1717/11 May 1718:   John SIMMONS
- wife Elizabeth, sons James and John, daughter
Sarah. Ex: wife. Wit: Henry SMITH, Solomon KEATON,
James TOOLY.

3DB193   27 Jan 1709/5 Mar 1717:   Rachel BENSON
- daughter Mary OGRADY, daughter Elizabeth, son William. Ex: William. Wit: Matthias GILES, Thomas
ATWOOD, Amy ATWOOD.

3DB201   5 Jun 1718/3 Sep 1718:   John SHIRLEY,
Sr. - sons John and George, wife Eliner, daughters
Mary and Alice NICHOLIS. Ex: wife and son George.
Wit: Thomas NORRIS, Mary KEELING, Mary LOOSLEY,
M. POWELL.

3DB206   11 Feb 1718/5 Nov 1718:   Edward OLD,
Sr. - sons Edward, Cockroft, Josias, John and James;
daughters Sarah and Margret. Ex: Cockroft. Wit:
Robert BELL, Ann BERRY, Solomon JONES.

3DB212   19 Feb 1718/4 Apr 1719:   Daniel HUT-
CHINGS - sons John and Nathaniel, wife Sarah. Ex:
wife and sons. Wit: William HUNTER, Richard DROUT,
Charles SAYER.

3DB217   31 Dec 1718/4 Mar 1718:   Samuel SHEP-
HERD - son John - certain things at ages 15 and 21,
Capt. William CRAFORD, wife Sarah. Ex: wife.

3DB220   17 Dec 1717/1 Apr 1719:   Richard DROUT -
daughter Ann HARVEY, sons John and Richard, daughter
Elizabeth MONTGOMARY. Ex: daughter Mary and Jehue
COCKROFT. Wit: Amy HUTCHINGS, George WEBLIN, Jehue
COCKROFT.

3DB223   18 Jan 1718/4 Mar 1718:   Owen MAGRAVY -
daughter Elizabeth, wife Mary, brother-in-law William
BENSON. Ex: wife Wit: Cason MOORE, Robert KEELING,
Cason SULLIVAN.

3DB227   2 Mar 1718/1 Apr 1719:   William HUNTER -
sons Thomas, James and John; wife Margret. Ex: wife,
and sons. Wit: Thomas EWELL, James DOLLAR, Charles
SAYER.

3DB227   14 Nov 1718/4 Mar 1718:   Matthias MOORE -
son Samuel, daughter Olive, wife Elizabeth. Ex: wife.
Wit: John PALLETT, George MONTGOMARY.

3DB228   23 Nov 1718/1 Apr 1719:   Jane LILBURN -
son William, daughter Jane EWELL. Ex: children. Wit:
Henry CHAPMAN.

3DB228   28 Mar 1719/6 May 1719:   John PALLETT -
son Mathew, daughter Elizabeth. Ex: two brothers-in-
law William ELLEGOOD and John COCKROFT. Wit: Christopher BURROUGH, Robert CARTWRIGHT, Adam LOVETT.

3DB229   10 Jan 1710/6 May 1719:   Thomas HARVEY,
Sr. - daughter Margret; sons Morris, Thomas and William; daughter Mary BURROUGH; sons John and Francis;
daughter Sarah; wife Katherine. Ex: son Thomas. Wit:
Joseph GOODAKER, Richard HOSKINS, Richard DROUT.

3DB229 14 Mar 1718/6 May 1719: John PURVINE -
Thomas PURVINE son of Lewis, brother Lewis. Ex:
brother Lewis. Wit: Lancaster LOVET, Thomas PHIL-
LIPS, Richard CROMPTON.

3DB229 6 Apr 1719/6 May 1719: Sarah CLOUSE -
Jonathan WALKE, son-in-law Anthony WALKE, daughter
Susannah THOROWGOOD, her daughter Pembrook, daughter
Margret, Cason son of Cason MOORE, Henry son of
Henry MOORE, sons Cason MOORE and Henry MOORE,
grandson James LAMOUNT. Ex: sons. Wit: Anthony
WALKE, Margret MOSELEY.

3DB230 14 Apr 1719/6 May 1719: William PEAD,
Sr. - sons John, William and Lemuel, daughters Mary
WILDER, Martha LOWERY, Dinah, Elizabeth and Jacomin.
Ex: Lemuel. Wit: John GRIFIN, Sarah MCDANIEL.

3DB231 22 Feb 1718/6 May 1719: Edward MOSELEY,
Jr. - wife Dinah, illegitimate son Robert MOSELEY,
sister Sarah POOLE, brother Palmer. Ex: wife. Wit:
Jehue COCKROFT, Richard DROUTT.

3DB232 ---/12 Apr 1719: Timothy DENNIS - wife
Ann, Thomas SNAILE son of my now wife, Elizabeth
CUDDEL. Ex: wife. Wit: John CANNON, Thomas GARROTT,
Richard CROMPTON.

3DB232 9 Apr 1719/6 May 1719: John CARROWAY,
Jr. - sons Edward, John and Thomas; daughters Eliza-
beth and Ann. Ex: Edward and John. Wit: Thomas HAYES,
Timothy DENNIS, Richard CROMPTON.

3DB233 6 May 1719: William ATWOOD to brother
John ATWOOD deed of gift of 12 acres. Wit: Jonathan
GODFREY, Robert KEELING. Richard CROMPTON.

3DB249 20 May 1719: Sarah BELL deed of gift
to James LEAMOUNT. Wit: John MACKIE, Anthony GUIL-
BERT.

3DB250 14 May 1719: John HUTCHINGS, mariner
to brother Nathaniel HUTCHINGS 75 acres in Little
Creek given him by late father Daniel HUTCHINGS.
Wit: John IVY, Anthony MOSELEY, George WEBLIN.

3DB252 20 Jun 1719: Anthony WALKE deed of gift
to children Jonathan and Margaret. Wit: Katherine
WALKE, Tully SMYTH, Charles SAYER.

3DB274 2 Sep 1719: Anthony WALKE, elder to
cozen Anthony son of brother Thomas deed of gift.
Wit: Edward MOSELEY, Charles SAYER.

3DB257 30 Apr 1719/3 Jan 1719: Lemuel HOLMES
- sons John, Lemuel, William and Henry; daughter
Dinah CHAPMAN wife of James; daughters William and
Amy. Ex: Henry HOLMES, Henry CHAPMAN. Wit: Henry
CHAPMAN, Henry HOLMES.

3DB258 16 May 1718/3 Jun 1719: John THOROW-
GOOD - son John, wife Pembrook, daughter Margret,
sister Mary, mother Margret SAYER, father-in-law
Charles SAYER, brother Arthur. Ex: wife, Thomas
WALKE and Charles SAYER. Wit: Thomas THOROWGOOD,
Francis THOROWGOOD, Charles SAYER.

3DB259   29 Jun 1710/3 Jun 1719:   Edward DAVIS - sons John, Edward, Thomas and William; grandson Edward SHARP, son-in-law Nicholas WILLIS; wife Hester. Ex: wife and son John. Wit: Richard CORBITT, Nicholas WILLIS, Mary WILLIS.

3DB260   4 May 1719/3 Jun 1719:   Adam THOROWGOOD - wife Mary, child wife goes with, nephew Adam son of brother William, Mary daughter of brother William, John son of brother Argal, three godchildren Mary, Ann and Margaret daughters of John THOROWGOOD, dec. and Elizabeth SAYER, brother William. Ex: wife and brother William. Wit: Patience THOROWGOOD, Elizabeth TENANT, Charles SAYER.

3DB260   11 Mar 1718/3 Jun 1719:   Benjamin BURROUGH - son Robert, wife Frances, son Arthur, daughter Elizabeth. Ex: wife. Wit: Christopher BURROUGH, Arthur BLAKE, Joseph SMITH.

3DB261   12 Apr 1719/3 Jun 1719:   John WEBLIN - son John, daughter Mary, wife Mary. Ex: brothers George and William. Wit: Robert MURDEN, Charles NORRIS.

3DB261   23 Apr 1719/3 Jun 1719:   Henry WOODHOUSE Elder - eldest son Phillip, younger son William, wife Elizabeth, daughter Mary. Ex: wife. Wit: Francis WOODHOUSE, John CUTH, John CORNICK.

3DB268   4 Aug 1719:   Sarah SHEPHERD deed of gift to son John. Wit: Thomas WALKE, Anthony WALKE, Peter TAYLOR.

3DB275   1 Sep 1719:   Richard SMITH Elder to son Thomas 100 acres in Blackwater. Wit: Willoughby MERCHANT, Richard CORBETT, Sarah SOLLEY.

3DB275   15 Apr 1719/2 Sep 1719:   James DAUGE - sons John, Richard and William (the New Plantation), daughters Mary, Macena and Nowdina, daughter Jacqueline CANNON; sons James and Peter (land in Currituck), wife Mary. If James does not come within six years then his share to Richard and Peter. Ex: wife and her brother John BONNEY. Wit: William BONNEY, Edward BONNEY.

3DB276   8 May 1719/5 Aug 1719:   Robert BRAY - wife Jacomin, son Plomer, daughter Mary, brother-in-law John WISHARD. Ex: wife. Wit: Edward BRAY, Mary WISHART.

3DB276   13 May 1719/5 Aug 1719:   John DAULEY - sons John (land in Muddy Creek called George's Quarter), William (Sasafras Ridge), Thomas (land on Broken Ridge and White Oak Plain), Henry and Dennis; daughters Elizabeth WOODHOUSE, Mary FOUNTAIN and Margret; granddaughters Mary FOUNTAIN and Mary WOODHOUSE, wife Mary. Ex: wife. Wit: Edward CANNON, Sr., Robert HUTCHINSON, Edward CANNON.

3DB278 22 Apr 1719/2 Sep 1719: Horatio WOOD-
HOUSE elder - son Horatio, daughters Mary THOROWGOOD,
Sarah, Olive and Elizabeth; wife Lucia; John MACKIE,
nephew Horatio son of brother John. Ex: wife and
Anthony WALKE. Nephew Henry son of brother Henry to
assist her. Wit: Robert KINGMAN, Henry MOORE, John
MACKIE.

3DB285 --=/2 Mar 1719: Francis SHIPP - noncupative will - all to Elizabeth FENTRIS. Wit: Thomas
WILES, Nathaniel NICKLES.

3DB293 25 Sep 1719/2 Dec 1719: George WARRING-
TON - son Clifton, wife Sarah, daughters Elizabeth
and Martha. Ex: wife and son. Wit: Willoughby
MARCHANT, Thomas DOBBS, Thomas OLDES.

3DB294 18 Nov 1719: Lawrence BRINDLE to Edward GUISBORN for 14 lbs. 200 acres - part of a tract
held by my father Lawrence. Wit: Thomas RICHARDS,
Thomas ALBRITTON.

3DB296 15 Oct 1719/6 Jan 1719: Robert CART-
WRIGHT - sons William, Thomas and John (land in Nuce
River), wife grandson William COTTEN; daughters
Sarah KEELING, Ann and Frances. Ex: sons William
and John. Wit: Benedict HORSINGTON, John CARTWRIGHT,
John TURNER.

3DB296 3 Feb 1719: Maximillian BOUSH and wife
Mary late relict of Jonathan SAUNDERS quit claim
unto John SAUNDERS, mariner, son and heir of Jonathan 100 acres called Kendalls Island. Wit: Reodolphus MALBONE, Job KEMP.

3DB297 5 Dec 1719: John NICKLES to Lewis
BAKER for 5 shillings 60 acres called Lyons Quarter
given NICKLES by his father's last will. Wit: George
SHIRLEY, Moses FENTRIS, Aron FENTRIS.

3DB299 27 Nov 1719/3 Feb 1719: George POOLE -
sons Richard and William, wife Hester, son-in-law
Adam HAYES and daughter Mary his wife, grandson
George SMITH, Robert and Blandina RICHMOND, daugh-
ters Elizabeth and Sarah. Ex: wife and son Rihchard.
Wit: Griffin FLOYD, George MUNTGUMARY, Richard CROMP-
TON.

3DB303 17 Feb 1719: Lucy WOODHOUSE deed of gift
to son Horatio, daughters Sarah and Elizabeth. Wit:
Lewis CONNER, William CAPPS.

3DB314 5 Apr 1720: Mary PITTS to son Thomas
deed of gift. Wit: John MACKIE, William CUSTIS.

3DB315 3 May 1720: David and Faith SCOTT to
Thomas SCOTT for 5 shillings 220 acres - part of
land left David by his father Thomas. Wit: Henry
SPRATT, Mathew GODFREY, Jeremiah LANGLEY.

3DB318 2 May 1720: Ann FENTRIS power of attorney
to son Moses to recover residue of James FENTRIS. Wit:
Anthony WALKE, Tully SMYTH.

3DB321   12 Jan 1718/19/6 Apr 1720:   George
MARSH - daughter Sarah WARD, daughter Elizabeth
CAPPS, daughter Jane KELLEY and her husband Charles,
grandson John KELLEY, grandson George WARD, grandson
Richard CAPPS, daughter Frances. Ex: Frances. Wit:
John MOY, Charles KENSEY, John HARRIES.

3DB321   18 Feb 1719/6 Apr 1720:   Mary LINTON -
Henry and William FITZGERALD sons of William and
Margaret FITZGERALD, sister Margret FITZGERALD,
full part of what was to be divided between her
and brother James LINTON. Wit: Elizabeth THOROW-
GOOD, Rosaner FITZGERALD, Solomon SHEAN.

3DB322   ---/6 Apr 1720:   Richard CAPPS - sons
William, John, James, Lewis, Thorowgood and Richard;
daughters Elizabeth BRINSON, Phillis and Ann; wife
Margret. Ex: wife. Wit: Edward GUISBORN, Dennis
DAULEY.

3DB322   27 Nov 1711/6 Apr 1720:   Stephen PEW
- sons Hugh and Stephen, wife Mary, each of my daughters. Ex: wife. Wit: John EDWARDS, Hugh WHITEHURST,
John WHITEHURST.

3DB322   15 Feb 1719/6 Apr 1720:   William ATTWOOD
- daughter Frances, wife Elizabeth, brother Thomas.
Ex: wife and brother. Wit: Alexander LEGGET, Elizabeth BENSON, Richard CROMPTON.

3DB323   12 Feb 1719/6 Apr 1720:   John RICHMOND
- brothers Anthony, Robert, George and William;
Thomas ATTWOOD, Richard CROMPTON. Ex: brother Robert. Wit: Isabell LOVETT, Robert KEELING, William
BENSON.

3DB323   7 Mar 1719/6 Apr 1720:   John ATTWOOD -
sons Francis, John, Edward and Thomas; daughters
Betty, Mary and Lucy; brother Thomas; Isaac PLEAD-
GER. Ex: wife and son Francis. Wit: Solomon MOSHER,
William CLARK, Richard CROMPTON

3DB324   21 Jan 1719/6 Apr 1720:   Cason MOORE -
sons Cason and William, wife Frances, daughters Sarah,
Elizabeth and Frances, Lewis PURVINE. E x: wife and
brother Henry. Wit: Thomas ATTWOOD, William ATTWOOD,
Martin BURRAS, Richard CROMPTON.

3DB325   3 Jun 1719/6 Apr 1720:   George BUSH -
son George, wife, my children. Ex: wife. Wit:
Willoughby MERCHANT, Anthony WALKE, Alexander LEGGET·
3DB325   6 Mar 1719/6 Apr 1720:   Thomas ATWOOD -
brother John, sister Amy LEGGET, John's son Francis,
cozens Mary WOODHOUSE and Elizabeth ATWOOD, Edward,
Thomas and John son of John, cozen Horatio WOODHOUSE,
John WOODHOUSE; Mary RUTLAND daughter of William.
Ex: brother John and Alexander LEGGET. Wit: William
RICHMOND, Jacomin WATERMAN, Richard CROMPTON.

3DB327 2 May 1720: Jehue COCKROFT and wife
Martha one of daughters of Mathew PALLET to John
ACKISS for 12 lbs. 50 acres - part of a tract gran-
ted Mathew PALLET known as Holland. Wit: Robert
KINGMAN, Mark POWELL.

3DB330 15 May 1720/1 Jun 1720: John FLABORN -
Cason MOORE, Henry MOORE. Ex: Henry. Wit: Dennis
CANNON, Cason MOORE.

3DB331 13 Mar 1715/6/1 Jun 1720: Richard
JONES of Knots Island - wife Rachel, sons Cornel-
ius and Richard, daughter Ann (Hickory Island),
six children Richard, Elizabeth, Sarah, Rebecah,
Jane and Leah. Ex: wife and son Richard. Wit:
John MALBON, Henry WHITE, Robert HUTCHINSON.

3DB337 12 Mar 1718/9/3 Aug 1720: Job BROOKS -
sons Job, John, Henry and Noah; daughter Ruth, wife.
Ex: wife. Wit: John ASHBY, Robert WOODS, Elizabeth
HILL.

3DB338 7 Sep 1720: Mary DAULEY deed of gift
to children John, Margret, Thomas, William and Henry.
Wit: M. BOUSH, Luke MOSELEY, Jabis BIGGS.

3DB346 4 Jan 1720: Robert VAUGHAN - deed to
son Robert, daughters Sarah and Ruth. Wit: Christopher BURROUGH, Peter TAYLOR, Charles SAYER.

3DB357 6 Dec 1720: Ann DENNIS deed to children
Thomas SNAILE, Elizabeth SNAILE, Ann SNAILE, Pem-
brook SNAILE (dec. husband Timothy DENNIS). Wit:
William LILBURN, William FITZGERALD.

3DB350 3 Oct 1720/7 Dec 1720: George HANCOCK -
brothers William and Ashwell; sons George and Hillary;
daughters Frances, Mary and Elizabeth; Lemuel THELA-
BALL; cozen Mary WISHARD. Ex: brother William and
Lemuel THELABALL. Wit: Henry HOLMES, Charles SAYER,
Margaret HUNTER.

3DB363 12 Oct 1720/4 Jan 1720: Richard CORBET -
sons John and Richard, daughters Abigall and Mary,
wife Frances, Thomas WILLIAMSON son of John. Ex:
wife. Wit: Sarah SOLLEY, Tully SMYTH, Elizabeth
SMYTH.

3DB366 30 Jan 1719/7 Sep 1720: George HANCOCK -
sons John and Robert; wife Barbara, daughters Mary,
Elizabeth and Barbara. Ex: wife. Wit: Joseph WHITE,
John RICHMOND, Richard CROMPTON.

3DB366 5 Feb 1710/1/1 Feb 1710: John STIREING -
sons John, Richard, George; three youngest children.
Ex: John BRINSON, Sr. and brother George. Wit: Luke
MOSELEY, Jacomin WATERMAN, Amey WATERMAN.

3DB382 16 Jan 1720/3 May 1721: John WHITE -
wife Elizabeth, daughter Mary, child wife goes with.
Ex: wife and brother Hugh. Wit: John SHIRLEY, William BROCK, Henry WHITEHURST, Jr.

3DB382   20 Jan 1721/3 May 1721:   Richard NICKLES
- sons Willis and Nathaniel, wife Martha. Ex: wife.
Wit: Anthony WEBB, Thomas WILES, Nathaniel NICKLES.

3DB383   27 Jan 1719/20/7 Jun 1721:   John EDMUNS
- sons William, John and Abell, daughter Elizabeth,
wife Mary. Ex: wife. Wit: John MURRAY, Sr., Hugh
PEW, David SCOTT.

3DB385   12 Mar 1720/5 Jul 1721:   Henry FITZ-
GERALD - sons John and Henry, daughter Margret,
wife Mary. Ex: wife. Wit: John HARPER, Gload
WHITCHARD.

3DB386   10 Feb 1719/20/5 Jul 1721:   James WHITE-
HURST, Sr. - sons James, John and Thomas; daughter
Sarah BAKER, granddaughter Dinah WHITEHURST daughter
of dec. son William; granddaughter Sarah BAKER;
daughter Elizabeth; wife Sarah. Wit: Henry WHITE-
HURST, Hugh WHITEHURST, John WHITEHURST.

3DB386   20 Jan 1720/5 Jul 1721:   James WHITE-
HURST, Jr. - sons James, Anthony and Godfrey, daugh-
ter Mary CARROWAY, wife Mary; wight children Eliza-
beth, James, William, Dinah, Thomas, Solomon and
Anthony. Ex: wife and son James. Wit: Thomas WHITE-
HURST, Thomas CARROWAY, Elizabeth WHITEHURST.

3DB400   4 Sep 1721:   Evan and Dinah JONES deed
to children Evan, Thomas, Martha and Gwinefreed.
Wit: Edward MOSELEY, John MOSELEY.

3DB413   6 Jun 1722:   Deposition of Edward MOSE-
LEY, Arthur BLAKE and George BOOTH that William WEST
who lives at North River is the son of William WEST,
Sr. of Pequimanes, NC and wife Susannah daughter of
William CHICHESTER.

3DB433   7 Oct 1721/6 Dec 1721:   Thomas EWELL -
sons James, Solomon and Thomas, wife, daughter Mary.
Overseers: Thomas WALKE and brother-in-law William
LILBURN. Wit: Thomas WISHARD, William DANIEL.

3DB434   ---/3 Jan 1721:   Henry SNAILE, Sr. -
grandchildren Elizabeth SNAILE, Henry SNAILE and
Mary WHITEHURST; sons Henry and John; Richard COOK;
Rose COOK, son-in-law Batson WHITEHURST. Ex: son
Henry and son-in-law. Wit: Richard COOK, Rose COOK.

3DB435   15 Feb 1721/7 Mar 1721:   Solomon JONES -
daughter Susannah (land father Evan JONES gave wife
Susannah), son-in-law Edward LEAMOUNT, son-in-law
Henry LEAMOUNT, son-in-law Thomas LEAMOUNT, Ex:
wife. Wit: William CAPPS, John MACKIE, Robert KING-
MAN.

3DB436   24 Jan 1721/2/4 Apr 1722:   Thomas ETHE-
RINGTON - son John MACKLAN, Sr., grandson John GRIN-
THO, wife Joan. Ex: wife. Wit: Robert HUTCHINSON,
Peter MALBONE, James LEAMOUNT.

3DB436   19 Aug 1721/1 Nov 1721:   Adam LOVET -
son William, daughter Elizabeth, unborn child. Ex:
wife. Wit: Henry WOODHOUSE, Adam KEELING, John
LOVETT.

3DB437 3 Apr 1721/1 Nov 1721: Richard PLUMTON -
Winifried BROCK wife of John BROCK, wife Sarah. Wit:
Margret SAYER, Mary THOROWGOOD, Charles SAYER.

3DB437 18 Jun 1720/4 Apr 1722: Peter GORNTO -
brother John (Bare Quarter). Ex: brother. Wit:
Randolph SPENCER, Elizabeth GILDING, John BONNEY.

3DB443 5 Jun 1722: George BOOTH deed of gift
to sons John and George. Wit: Richard JONES, Andrew
PEACOCK.

3DB445 10 May 1722/6 Jun 1722: Clifton WAR-
TINGTON - daughter Bettey, Amos CUTERALL, wife Mary.
Ex: wife. Wit: Moses PRESCOTT, John CUMMING.

3DB448 10 Mar 1721/4 Jul 1722: Thomas COR-
PREW - wife Elizabeth, son Thomas, daughter Abiah
CHURCH. Ex: wife. Wit: Lawrence DOYLEY, Mathew
GODFREY, Henry SOUTHERN.

3DB448 5 Feb 1720/1 Aug 1722: James CASON -
sons Thomas, James and William; daughters Elizabeth
WHITEHURST, Susannah MOORE and Dyner WILBER; grandson Cason MOORE. Ex: William WEST. Wit: William
WEST, William BROWN.

3DB458 5 Sep 1722: Alexander LEGGET deed of
gift to son Anthony. Wit: William BENSON, Richard
CROMPTON, Jane CROMPTON.

3DB457 19 Feb 1721/2/7 Nov 1722: Thomas RAY-
LEY - sons John, Thomas, Edward and James, wife Mary.
Ex: brother-in-law John MOY. Wit: John GRIFEN,
Joseph SUGG.

3DB458 5 Sep 1722: John MALBONE deed of gift
to sons Peter and John. Wit: Robert VAUGHAN, Reodolphus MALBONE.

3DB469 14 Feb 1719/2 Jan 1722: Thomas DUDLEY -
wife Frances; sons Ambross, William, Thomas and
Richard; daughters Frances MUNDEN, Joyce GOODAKER
and Dorathy. Ex: wife. Wit: John HARPER, Mary
HARPER, Mary LEFESLEY.

3DB471 5 Sep 1722: Inventory of Thomas HEATH
by Richard EILAND, Robert VAUGHAN, Thorowgood KEELING.

3DB472 2 Jan 1722: Martha NICHOLAS deed of
gift to sons Willis and Nathaniel. Wit: Nathaniel
NICKLES, Anthony WEBB.

3DB475   Feb 1722/3: William KEELING to Thomas
WALSTONE for 5 shillings 100 acres which I have by
death of brother Robert given by father Alexander
KEELING. Wit: John GORNTO, John MOY.

3DB476 2 Jan 1722: Appraisement of estate of
Thomas HALL by John HARPER, John SMITH, Bartholomew
WILLIAMSON.

3DB478 12 Sep 1722/6 Feb 1722: Tully EMPEROR -
grandson Thomas MOSELEY (son of daughter Mary WHITE-
HURST), granddaughter Frances MOSELEY, grandson William ACKISS, grandson Tully MOSELEY, grandson Emperor

MOSELEY, daughter Eliza MOSELEY, granddaughters
Eliza and Frances MOSELEY daughters of Mary WHITE-
HURST, granddaughter Sarah ACKISS, grandson Joseph
MOSELEY; daughter Ann WHEELER, daughter Sarah ACKISS,
wife. Ex: son-in-law Henry WHITEHURST and William
ACKISS. Wit: Anthony WALKE, John MURRAY, Adam BEL-
LEMY.

3DB480 24 Sep 1722/2 Jan 1722: Robert DEAR-
MORE - son Robert's children, grandson Lemuel JAMES.
Ex: Christopher BURROUGH and Arthur BLAKE. Wit:
Samuel BROCK and William CAPPS

3DB481 4 Jun 1716/2 Jan 1722: Evan JONES -
eldest son Solomon; sons Patrick, Evan and Thomas;
daughters Elizabeth MALBONE, Dinah LURRY, Margaret
PURDY, Ruth SHEPHERD, Mary, Martha and Winifried;
wife Dinah. Ex: wife. Wit: Joseph WICKER, Joseph
SAUNDERSON.

3DB482 27 Nov 1722/6 Feb 1722: Edward LAND -
wife Mary, sons Renatus and Edward, grandson Edward
son of Renatus, grandson William, granddaughter Mary,
daughter Mary BRINSON, daughter Sarah, Francis LAND
son of cousen Francis. Ex: son Edward. Wit: Francis LAND, Job GASKING.

3DB482 30 Nov 1722/8 Feb 1722: Thomas LOVET -
wife Martha. Ex: wife. Wit: Paul RIGBY, Francis
SPANN, William GILDING

3DB482 6 Feb 1722: Inventory of Lawrence
BRIDGES by William ELLEGOOD, Francis WOODHOUSE,
William CAPPS.

3DB483 4 Jan 1722/3 Apr 1723: Ann HEATH -
grandson James HEATH, Thomas HEATH son of James,
granddaughters Eliza EILAND, Eliza HEATH, Jane
EILAND, John HEATH. Ex: Francis MORSE. Wit: Wes-
well ANDERSON, Abigail GILDING.

3DB484 5 Mar 1723: George GRIFFEN and wife
Rose to James LANGLEY for 5 shillings 50 acres -
part of a patent of my father Charles GRIFFEN.
Wit: James NIMMO, Thomas HUNTER.

3DB485 6 Mar 1722: Richard STONE to brother
John 150 acres in North Woods, if without heirs to
brother George. Wit: William ELLEGOOD, John SNAILE.

3DB485 1 Apr 1723: James HEATH to brother
Robert HEATH of Coratuck deed of gift of 200 acres
known as Eagles Nest. Wit: Richard EILAND, Andrew
PEACOCK.

3DB497 1 Jun 1723: John and Sarah HOLMES to
William HOLMES for 5 lbs 1/3 of tract in Little
Creek belonging to John HOLMES, Sr. dec. Wit:
John SMITH, James EWELL.

3DB501 3 Jul 1723: John MOSELEY to son Francis
MOSELEY for 6 shillings 50 acres. Wit: Thomas WALKE,
Anthony WALKE.

3DB504   7 Aug 1723: Division of property of
Adam THOROWGOOD - children Francis, Margret and John
- by Robert KINGMAN, Francis LAND, John SMITH.

3DB507   7 Aug 1723: Horatio WOODHOUSE, mariner
to pay Horatio, son of John WOODHOUSE. Wit: William
ELLEGOOD, Reodolphus MALBONE, William CAPPS.

3DB507   7 Aug 1723: Elizabeth BRINSON deed of
gift to children John WILLIAMS, Margret WILLIAMS,
Elizabeth WILLIAMS and Lemuel JAMES. Wit: Charles
SAYER, Arthur SAYER.

3DB520   1 Sep 1721/6 Nov 1723: Richard WIL-
LIAMSON - sons Roger, John, Bartholomew and George;
George's daughter Mary; daughter Mary BERRY wife of
Robert BERRY; daughter Sarah wife of Mathew MATHIAS;
grandson Caleb son of daughter Ann WHITEHURST wife
of Hugh; wife Mary. Ex: Bartholomew and George.
Wit: Anthony WEBB, George SHIRLEY, Mary SHIRLEY.

3DB521   19 Oct 1723/6 Nov 1723: Peter OLIVER -
George KEMPE. Wit: James NIMMO, Anthony IVY, Robert
HOLMES.

3DB521   19 Jan 1722/3/2 Oct 1723: John MOY -
daughter Jane BISHOP. Ex: son Richard MOY. Wit:
William SUGG, Jabis BIGGS.

3DB521   11 Aug 1722/5 Feb 1723: Margaret MOSE-
LEY - son Francis, grandson William, daughter Margaret,
friend Mrs. Margret SAYER. Wit: Barbara SAYER, Margaret SAYER.

3DB528   1 Jan 1723: Edward CANNON to son Edward
deed of gift of 115 acres, half of tract known as
Wollford. Wit: John CORNICK, William VESE.

3DB528   1 Jan 1723: Edward CANNON to son Denis
CANNON 100 acres - other half of Wollford. Wit: John
CORNICK, William VESE.

3DB529   10 Oct 1723/1 Jan 1723: Edward CARROWAY -
brother Thomas, sister Ann, sister Sarah, brother John.
Ex: John Wit: Charles WILLIAMSON, James CARROWAY.

3DB529   19 Nov 1723/1 Jan 1723: John ATWOOD -
sister Mary, brother Edward, uncle Alexander LEGGETT.
Ex: uncle. Wit: Richard CAPPS, William BRINSON.

3DB530   16 Jan 1722/4 Dec 1723: Tully SMYTH -
sons Tully and Charles, wife Elizabeth, daughters
Elizabeth, Ann and Frances, godson Charles SAYER.
Ex: son Charles. Wit: Thomas DELEMARE, William
POOLE, Easter POOLE

3DB531   7 Sep 1719/4 Dec 1723: Thomas FRANKLIN -
sons William, Thomas, Daniel, Richard, Nathaniel and
John; wife Sarah. Wit: John BONNEY, Jr., William
PURDY.

3DB532   4 Dec 1723/1 Jan 1723: James READ -
son Elisha, Willoughby MERCHANT. Ex: Willoughby
MERCHANT. Wit: Christopher MERCHANT, Josias JONES.

3DB532　22 Mar 1722/5 Feb 1723:　Thomas WALKE - sons Anthony and Thomas, wife Katherine, daughters Elizabeth and Katherine.　Ex: brother Anthony WALKE. Wit: D.A. MCCLENAHAN, Charles SAYER, Edward BRAY.

3DB532　10 Dec 1723/4 Mar 1723:　William THOROW- GOOD - sons Argal and Adam, daughter Mary, wife Pati- ence.　Ex: wife and Thomas THOROWGOOD.　Wit: Jacob MACLOUD, Ann TREVETHAN.

3DB533　4 Mar 1723/1 Apr 1724:　John KEMPE, elder - cozen John WILLIAMSON, cozens George KEMPE, Roger WILLIAMSON and John WILLIAMSON, sister Eliza- beth SMITH, cozen Mary WISHARD, cozen Ann COOPER wife of Thomas, cozen James KEMPE, cozen Thomas WISHARD elder, cozen Mary daughter of George KEMPE, brother-in-law William SMITH.　Ex: Thomas WISHARD, elder and John WILLIAMSON.　Wit: Eliza WILLIAMSON, Samuel GRANBERRY, Anthony WALKE.

3DB542　12 Jul 1722:　John SEALEY to Edward GIZBOURN for 15 lbs. 50 acres in Blackwater which came to me from my grandfather John WHARTON.　Wit: John AIRES, William SUGG.

3DB558　4 May 1724:　Malbone SIMMONS and wife Mary deed of gift to sister-in-law Sarah JONES 35 acres on Knotts Island being part of a patent granted to my father-in-law Michaell JONES.　Wit: Francis WOODHOUSE, William CAPPS.

3DB562　30 May 1724/2 Sep 1724:　Horatio WOOD- HOUSE - friend Thomas DELEMARE, Hester WALSTONE, sister Elizabeth, other sisters, James EWELL, cusen Horatio son of John WOODHOUSE.　Ex: Anthony WALKE and Reodolphus MALBONE.　Wit: William CAPPS, Maxi- millian BOUSH, Jr.

3DB572　3 Oct 1724:　Susannah THOROWGOOD deed of gift to children John and Pembrook.　Wit: Anthony WALKE, Elizabeth WALKE, Honour DEARMORE.

DEED BOOK FOUR

4DB1   10 Sep 1730/7 Oct 1730:   Robert BERRY -
wife Mary, sons Richard and Robert, all my children.
Ex: wife.   Wit: Bartholomew WILLIAMSON, Sarah MATH-
YAS.

4DB6   21 Jan 1724/7 Apr 1725:   George SMITH -
brother Francis GASKING and sister Easter HAYES all
my estate in the hands of my father-in-law Job GAS-
KING.   Ex: father-in-law and grandmother Easter POOLE.
Wit: William POOLE, Sarah POOLE, Henry HOLMES.

4DB8   3 Feb 1724:   William CARROWAY and wife Ann
and John DAULEY and wife Mary, two of daughters of
William MOORE to Daniel FRIZELL for 17 lbs. two-
thirds part of 100 acres in the Western SHORE.   Wit:
Francis MORSE, Thomas LAWSON, Thomas CARROWAY, James
CARROWAY.

4DB9   16 Apr 1724/8 Feb 1724:   John MCLOUD -
sons Daniel, John and Jacob, wife, daughter Mary
COOPER.   Ex: son Jacob.   Wit: Richard ADAMS, Charles
SAYER.

4DB11   21 Nov 1724/3 Feb 1724:   John LAMBART -
William, Andrew and Thomas MORGAN, wife Jane.   Ex:
wife.   Wit: John BONNEY, Jr., Elizabeth MORRIS.

4DB13   3 Mar 1724:   William COTANCO and wife
Ann to Luke MOSELEY 50 acres in Dam Neck given by
will of Timothy DENNIS to Ann.   Wit: John MUNDON,
George WEBLIN.

4DB14   21 Feb 1721/3 Feb 1724:   John BONNEY, Sr.
- wife Mary, daughter Mary GORNTO, daughter Frances
(North end of Long Island), son John (remainder of
Long Island).   Ex: John.   Wit: Thomas RICHARDS, Denis
DAULEY.

4DB14   7 May 1724/4 Nov 1724:   Robert KINGMAN -
daughter Mary daughter of Mary KINGMAN alias SAUNDERS,
son (Ford of Pamplico), daughter Ann, Ann SCOTT, Mary
MOORE formerly Mary LOOSLY, Charles SAYER, Capt.
Francis LAND.   Ex: Charles SAYER and Capt. Francis
LAND.   Wit: William CLARK, Rebecca BAX, Richard
CROMPTON.

4DB30   4 Aug 1724:   Dinah JONES widow of Evan to
Thomas DUDLEY for 16 lbs. 99 acres on Knots Island
called Cartwright's Point.   Wit: Cornelius JONES,
Levi CROSSLEY, Malbone SIMMONS.

4DB31   28 Feb 1720/3 Nov 1725: Anthony IVY -
mother Ursula IVY, brothers Lemuel and George, sister
Sarah. Ex: mother. Wit: Joseph TOWLSON, John STUART,
William BIDDLES.

4DB45   28 Jun 1725:   Thomas CARROWAY of Eastern
Branch to William CARROWAY of North Woods for 5 shillings 100 acres at Borin's River given Thomas by his
father John. Wit: James ISDELL, William BROCK.

4DB47   5 May 1725/1 Sep 1725: John MOSELEY,
mariner - brother Francis, sister Ellen, cozen John
MOSELEY, sister Mary MALBONE, brother-in-law Reodolphus MALBONE. Wit: Amos MOSELEY, William CAPPS.

4DB52   30 Nov 1725: Alexander LEGGET to Thomas
LEGGET for 6 shillings 70 acres on Knots Island -
part of land given Alexander by will of John LEGGET.
Wit: Malbone SIMMONS, Charles MALBONE.

4DB54   5 Jan 1725: Ursula IVY to son-in-law
Samuel GRANBERRY and wife Alice and children Ursilla,
Alif, Elinor, Ann and Sarah 100 acres on SW side of
the Cyprus Swamp. Wit: James NIMMO, Arthur BLAKE.

4DB54   6 Feb 1725: John WHITEHURST to brother-
in-law John SMITH 15 acres in North Woods. Wit:
William LILBURN, Edward BRAY, Henry SNAILE.

4DB55   28 Jan 1725: Josias JONES of NC to Owen
JONES of Norfolk Co for 35 lbs. 130 acres in Black-
water patented by Francis JONES. Wit: William SENIOR,
Francis LAND, James TOOMOTH.

4DB57   11 Apr 1723/2 Mar 1725: Capt Richard
CHESHIRE of town of Norfolk being bound up the bay
on my sloop - son John land in Princess Anne Co,
daughters Sarah and Mary. Ex: Martha THRUSTON, Thomas WALKE, Anthony WALKE.

4DB59   19 Apr 1720/2 Mar 1725: William SMITH,
Jr. - sons George, William and John, wife Elizabeth,
daughters Martha and Elizabeth. Ex: wife. Wit:
Arthur BLAKE, Blandina MOSELEY, Elizabeth BURROUGH.

4DB62   4 May 1726: Elizabeth CORNICK deed of
gift to children William, Joel, Nimrod, Endimion,
Henry and Prudence - property I had of my father
Henry WOODHOUSE. Wit: Solomon KEATON, John GUISBORN.

4DB64   7 May 1726/6 Jul 1726: William ELLEGOOD -
sons Jacob, Mathew, Henry, John (Timber Neck) and William; daughters Martha, Mary and Sarah. Ex: son Jacob
and son-in-law Thomas HARVEY. Wit: James TENANT, John
COCKROFT, William CAPPS.

4DB66   3 Aug 1726: Elizabeth BROCK deed of gift
to brother Henry BRINSON 100 acres in Dam Neck called
Dobs Plantation left her by father. Wit: Henry BRIN-
SON, Elizabeth ALBRITTON.

4DB67   3 Aug 1726: William DYER deed of gift to
sons William and John, daughter Sarah OAKHAM. Wit:
William DAUGE, Charles SAYER, Nathaniel SENECA.

4DB68 20 Jan 1714/7 Sep 1726: Sampson TREVE-
THAN of Penzance in Cornwall power of attorney to
wife Ann and friends Christopher COCKE and Charles
SAYER. Wit: Dan HAWKEY Mayor of Penzance.

4DB74 9 Oct 1726/7 Dec 1726: Henry WHITEHURST
- wife Mary; sons Robert, Henry and Samuel; daughter
Sarah. Wit: Francis MOSELEY, William COCKROFT, James
PAIRTREE.

4DB75 20 Mar 1727/8/1 May 1728: Robert LAND -
wife Phebe; sons Francis, Richard, Renatus, Edward
and Robert; daughters Sarah, Mary and Phebe. Ex:
wife and son Francis. Wit: John WHITEHURST, Elizabeth FRIZELL.

4DB79 15 Sep 1726/2 Nov 1726: Cason MOORE -
wife Ann, son John (Long Island). Ex: wife and her
brother Henry WOODHOUSE. Wit: Thomas HAYNES, William COX, James CONDON.

4DB84 3 Oct 1726/7 Dec 1726: Thomas COOPER -
daughter Lydia, wife Ann. Ex: wife. Wit: George
KEMPE, Anna HANCOCK.

4DB84 14 Oct 1726: Division of property of
William SMYTH - Francis MOSELEY and wife Margret,
eldest daughter of said dec. pay to other two sisters. Wit: Reodolphus MALBONE, Thomas HAYNES,
Charles SAYER.

4DB86 2 Nov 1726: Mary BONNEY deed of gift to
sons John, Henry, Thomas and William DAWLEY, daughter-
in-law Mary DAWLEY, daughters Mary FOUNTAIN and Margret CANNON. Wit: Robert HUTCHINSON, John BONNEY.

4DB86 ---/5 Oct 1726: George IVY - noncupative will - all to brother Lemuel. Wit: Robert
SMITH IVY.

4DB89 10 Dec 1726: William RUSSEL of NC son
of William RUSSEL and son-in-law of William HILYARD
to Thomas HAYNES for 35 lbs. 120 acres given by William HILYARD to father William RUSSEL. Wit: Jacob
ELLEGOOD, Robert RICHMOND, Adam KEELING, William
CAPPS.

4DB91 24 Aug 1726/1 Feb 1726: Susanah JONES -
sons James, Thomas, Edward and Henry LEAMOUNT, daughter Susanah JONES. Ex: sons Edward and John. Wit:
John CORNICK, Sarah BALL.

4DB92 ---/1 Feb 1726: Arthur BLAKE - daughter
Frances PAIRTREE, granddaughter Frances MOSELEY, son-
in-law James PAIRTREE, grandson Robert BURROUGH, son-
in-law John WILLIAMS, grandson James WILLIAMS, cozen
John BONNEY, four granddaughters Frances MOSELEY,
Elizabeth BURROUGH, Sarah BURROUGH and Elizabeth
WILLIAMS. Ex: two sons-in-law James PAIRTREE and
John WILLIAMS. Wit: William POOLE, Alexander
HARVEY.

4DB94 1 Feb 1726: George KEMPE deed of gift to son James - if no heirs to son John. Wit: Charles SAYER, Hillary MOSELEY.

4DB96 5 Jan 1726/7/5 Apr 1726: John ROBERTS - wife Mary. Ex: wife. Wit: John TURVILO, Thomas DAULLEY.

4DB98 26 Aug 1723/1 Mar 1726: Dinah HATTERS-LEY - mother Dorcas BROUGHTON. Ex: mother. Wit: Martha COCKROFT, Jehue COCKROFT.

4DB100 3 Feb 1726/1 Mar 1726: Thomas THOROW-GOOD - wife Mary, child wife goes with, brother Robert. Ex: wife. Wit: John THOROWGOOD, Charles SAYER, Elizabeth TENANT.

4DB101 23 Dec 1726/1 Mar 1726: James TENANT - wife Elizabeth, daughter Elizabeth, sons James and Samuel. Ex: wife, Charles SAYER and Anthony WALKE. Wit: Francis LAND, Thomas THOROWGOOD.

4DB101 3 Dec 1726/5 Apr 1726: George MONTGOMARY - sons George, John and Hugh, daughter Frances, wife Elizabeth. Ex: wife. Wit: Palmer MOSELEY, William COCKROFT.

4DB102 1 Jan 1726/5 Apr 1727: Edward BRAY - wife Mary; three daughters Elizabeth, Mary and Olive; child wife goes with. Ex: wife. Wit: Mary WISHARD, Amos MOSELEY.

4DB102 7 Mar 1726/7/5 Apr 1727: Thomas BROCK - daughters Sarah and Hester, son Henry. Ex: John MUNDEN, Cason BRINSON. Wit: Job BROOKS, Elizabeth BARFOOT.

4DB102 26 May 1727/2 Aug 1726: Hester WALSTON - granddaughters Rebecca SULLIVAN and Mary SMITH, son John SULLIVAN. Ex: son. Wit: John DAUGE, James LAMOUNT.

4DB105 3 Apr 1727: Capt. Edward MOSELEY deed of gift to son Hillary of 198 acres. Wit: William CAPPS, James NIMMO, William POOLE.

4DB114 21 Mar 1726/7/3 May 1727: John CORNICK - son Lemuel; daughters Frances WOODHOUSE, Mary WHITE, Alef WHITE, Elizabeth CANNON and Sarah; wife. Ex: wife and son-in-law Horace WOODHOUSE. Wit: Reodolphus MALBONE, Robert HUTCHINSON, Mary MALBONE.

4DB114 3 May 1727: Division of estate of William CONSALVO - sons William and John. Reodolphus MALBONE, William CAPPS.

4DB115 17 Mar 1726/3 May 1727: Francis THELA-BALL - sons James, Lemuel, Thomas (plantation in Norfolk Co.) and Lewis, wife Abigal. Ex: wife. Wit: Mathew GODFREY, Thomas TAYLOR, William NASH.

4DB115 14 Feb 1726/3 May 1727: Lemuel THELA-BALL - son Robert, wife Joyes, daughters Margret, Keziah and Mary. Ex: wife. Wit: William LILBURN, Francis THELABALL, John HOLMES.

4DB120   17 Feb 1726/7 Jun 1727:   Willoughby
MERCHANT of Blackwater - wife Elizabeth; sons Keader,
Caleb, Willoughby, Haberaniah, Gideon and Christo-
pher; daughters Jane and Elizabeth. Ex: wife and son
Christopher. Wit: William CORBELL, William GISBORNE,
Thomas DOBBS.
   4DB123   5 Dec 1725/2 Aug 1727:   William SMITH -
wife Elizabeth, sons John and James, all my children.
Wit: Francis MOSELEY, ____ MOSELEY.
   4DB125   Jun 1727:   Edward OLD heir and grandson
of Edward OLD for 2200 lbs. to John WITCHARD 200 acres -
southernmost part of a ridge of land known as Chincopen
Ridge patented by William CORNICK and given by will to
Francis MORSE and conveyed to Edward OLD the Elder.
Wit: Joel CORNICK, James HARRISON.
   4DB131   12 Jan 1726/7/5 Jul 1727:   Davis SCOTT -
sons Richard, Thomas and John; daughters Frances,
Margret and Mary; child wife goes with; wife Faith.
Ex: wife. Wit: John BOLITHOE, Daniel MCCLENAHAN,
Francis GERAM.
   4DB132   15 Nov 1691/15 Mar 1691:   John WHITE-
HURST of Norfolk Co - sons John and Hugh; daughters
Elizabeth and ___, wife Mary. Ex: wife. Wit: Henry
NICOLAS, Edward TRANTER, William LINTON, James WHITE-
HURST.
   4DB132   5 Sep 1717/4 Oct 1727:   Edward JAMES -
wife Mary, son Edward. brother John. Wit: Robert
HUTCHINSON, John MOY, John JAMES.
   4DB141   21 Aug 1727/1 Nov 1727:   William WICKER
of Knots Island - Willis WICKER, Mary and Aliff JONES
daughters of Richard JONES. Ex: Richard JONES. Wit:
Cornelius JONES, Andrew PEACOCK.
   4DB146   25 Mar 1727/1 Nov 1727:   George BULLOCK -
son-in-law John SIMPSON, wife Mary. Ex: son-in-law.
Wit: Thomas DUDLEY, John MOY.
   4DB147   9 Oct 1727/1 Nov 1727:   Joel CORNICK -
sons Henry, Endimion, Nimrod, William and Joel; daughter Pondance. Ex: Joel. Wit: James HARRISON, James
CONDON, Max BOUSH, Jr.
   4DB149   31 Oct 1727:   John and Mary DAULY and
John and Elizabeth JAMES, daughters and coadminis-
trators of William MOORE to John FENTRIS - two-thirds
part of 100 acres. Wit: Charles SAYER, Francis LAND.
   4DB151   1 Oct 1727:   John CORBET eldest son of
Richard CORBET for 6 shillings to Richard STONE 350
acres near Salmon's Bridge or Cyprus Run. Wit: Thomas
WHITEHURST, Hugh WHITEHURST, John WHITEHURST, William
NICHOLSON.
   4DB153   6 Dec 1727:   Richard and Hannah STONE to
brother John 150 acres in North Woods - if he dies to
brother George. Wit: Richard MOSELEY, John WISHARD.

4DB153 6 Dec 1727: Roger WILLIAMSON, son and heir of Richard WILLIAMSON, dec. to George WILLIAMSON for 50 shillings 15 acres in the Eastern Branch. Wit: Arthur SAYER, Bartholomew WILLIAMSON.

4DB154 1 Nov 1727: Mary WISHARD deed of gift to son John 50 acres known as Hogg Island. Wit: John SAUNDERS, Thomas HUNTER.

4DB158 15 Aug 1727/3 Apr 1728: Maximilian BOUSH the Elder - sons Samuel and Maximilian, uncle Col. Samuel BOUSH, John HOLLOWAY, godson Miximilian CALVERT, son Maximilian's daughter Mary. Ex: Maximilian and cozen Capt. Samuel BOUSH.

4DB167 23 Jan 1727/8/3 Apr 1728: James HEATH - sons James and Thomas, son-in-law Eustace STRIPES, wife Mary. Ex: wife. Wit: Francis MORSE, Andrew PEACOCK, John HEATH

4DB174 15 Nov'1727/1 May 1728: John GWIN - wife Margaret. Ex: wife. Wit: William GODFREY, Mary BRAY.

4DB173 28 ---/1 May 1728: Olive BRAY - daughter-in-law Mary BRAY, grandchildren Elizabeth and Plomer BRAY, Olive BRAY daughter of Edward. Ex: daughter-in-law Mary. Wit: Amos MOSELEY, Joyes ASHLY.

4DB182 4 Apr 1728/5 Jun 1728: Reodolphus MALBONE - sons Charles, Reodolphus and Francis; wife Mary; daughter Mary WOODHOUSE. Ex: wife. Wit: Francis MOSELEY, William CAPPS, Anthony MOSELEY.

4DB182 30 Mar 1725/5 Jun 1728: John ACKISS - sons William, John, Adam and Francis (land called Holland); wife Katherine; grandchildren William and Katherine children of William; grandchildren Margret and John EDWARDS, granddaughters Sarah and Jane daughters of John, Elizabeth daughter of Francis. Ex: wife. Wit: James TOOMOTH, Anthony WALKE.

4DB183 21 Apr 1728/5 Jun 1728: William CAPPS - sister Sarah BROCK, John BARFOOT son of Ambros, sister Mary JARVIS, William BARFOOT, Mary MALBONE widow of Reodolphus, Horatio WOODHOUSE, Abia COX, brother and sister Samuel and Sarah BROCK. Ex: brother-in-law Samuel BROCK. Wit: Charles MALBONE, Francis WOODHOUSE, Elizabeth SMITH, Jacob ELLEGOOD.

4DB187 4 Jun 1728: Appraisement of the estate of Caleb DROUT by William MCCLENAHAN, John THOROWGOOD and Lancaster LOVETT.

4DB193 3 Jun 1728/3 Jul 1728: Henry SIMMONS - sons George, Richard and Henry; wife Ann. Ex: wife. Wit: John BUTLER, Anthony BARNS, Luke MOSELEY.

4DB193 3 Jul 1728: Dinah WALSTONE deed of gift to son Thomas and daughter Ann. Wit: George WEBLIN, William BROCK.

4DB199   23 May 1728/7 Aug 1728:   Dennis DAULLEY -
sons John and Dennis, daughters Mary and Amy, brothers
John, Thomas, William and Henry, wife Amy. Ex: wife.
Wit: John TURVILO, Mary ROBERTS, John BONNEY.

4DB200   6 Aug 1728:   Mary HEATH deed of gift to
sons Jacobus and Robert, son-in-law James HEATH, Benoni HEATH and John LAWLEY.

4DB201   24 Apr 1728/7 Aug 1728:   John HERBERT -
sons Richard, Willoughby (land in Norfolk Co), John,
Thomas and Peter; wife Elizabeth; daughters Elizabeth BATCHELER, Mary SUGGS, Dinah, Margret, Violet
and Ann. Ex: wife and Thomas. Wit: William CORNICK,
Henry _____, Christopher PHILPOTT.

4DB202   11 Jun 1728/2 Oct 1728:   Elizabeth SMITH -
daughters Martha, Mary and Elizabeth; sons George,
William and John. Ex: Martha. Wit: Dorcas BROUGHTON
Thomas COCKROFT.

4DB203   20 Mar 1727/8/2 Oct 1728:   John MCCLA-
NAHAN - sons John, Thomas and Richard (BADLY TORN)
Wit: John DAUGE, Peter MALBONE, John MALBONE.

4DB210   24 Jan 1727/2 Oct 1728:   John CARROWAY -
granddaughter Sarah, sons William, James and Thomas;
daughters Dinah HORSINGTON, Ann WHITEHURST and Elizabeth WHITEHURST; wife Ann. Ex: son James. Wit:
Daniel MCCLENAHAN, Charles WILLIAMSON, Richard WHITE-
HURST.

4DB213   14 Jun 1728/6 Nov 1728:   Mary ROBERTS -
grandson Philip, William and Mary WOODHOUSE, daughter
Mary FOUNTAIN, grandson John FOUNTAIN, daughter Margret CANNON, son John DAULEY, four grandchildren
John, Dennis, Mary and Amy DAULEY, three youngest
sons Thomas, William and Henry DAULEY. Ex: son Thomas DAULEY. Wit: John TURVILO, William CAPPS.

4DB214   24 Nov 1728/4 Dec 1728:   Jehue COCKROFT -
son Thomas, daughters Mary, Frances, Elizabeth, Ann
and Sarah. Ex: son. Friends Nathaniel HUTCHINGS
and John HARPER to make division. Wit: Dorcas BROUGH-
TON, John HARPER.

4DB226   20 Nov 1728/1 Jan 1728/9:   Catran CREEDLE
- sons William and Francis, daughters Catran and Alisir.
Wit: James BANISTER, Thomas CAPTS, Rebeca BRINSON.

4DB227   21 Dec 1727/5 Feb 1728/9:   Richard JONES -
sons James, Richard and Solomon; daughters Aime and
Martha. Ex: Martha. Wit: John CARE. Dennis CARE.

4DB228   17 Dec 1728/5 Feb 1728/9:   Thomas WISH-
ARD - wife Mary; sons Thomas, George, William and
John; daughters Ann and Jacomin. Ex: wife and son
Thomas. Wit: Henry CHAPMAN, Abraham MILLS, William
WISHARD.

4DB232   3 Mar 1728/9:   Henry WHITE to sister
Elizabeth DUDLEY wife to Robert to fulfill desire of
my father Solomon WHITE of Coratuck, dec. 250 acres
on Knots Island. Wit: Solomon WHITE, John MORFE.

4DB235   ---/7 Jan 1729/30: Giles COLLINS -
John and Henry COLLINS. Wit: Elizabeth STANDLE,
Ann COLLINS.

4DB241   ---/2 Jun 1729: Thomas SCOTT - grand-
son Cason son of son Thomas, granddaughters Elizabeth
ALGREW, Ann daughter of Anthony MOSELEY, and Ann SIM-
MONS; son-in-law Anthony MOSELEY and daughter Frances
his wife. Ex: Anthony MOSELEY. Wit: Edward MOSELEY,
Amos MOSELEY, Palmer MOSELEY.

4DB254   14 Oct 1725/3 Sep 1729: Samuel STAR-
LING - Mary STARLING, James HEATH. Ex: James HEATH.
Wit: William GUILDING, Elizabeth JONES, Margret
STRIPES.

4DB272   4 Feb 1728/7 Jan 1729/30: James TOOLY -
son Adam, daughter Mary, daughter Elizabeth MORRIS,
son-in-law William MILLER, son-in-law John WHITEHEAD,
granddaughter Abia WHITEHEAD, daughter Rebecca MILLER,
granddaughter Liddy MILLER. Ex: Adam. Wit: William
CORBELL, Malbone SIMMONS, Ephraim JONES.

4DB279   19 Sep 1729/4 Mar 1729: Thomas SPRATT -
sons James, Thomas and Henry, wife Elizabeth, John
BONNEY, daughter Amy CANNON, daughters Mary and Isbill.
Ex: wife. Wit: Robert MASON, Edward MILLIAM.

4DB280   1 Apr 1730: Mary WISHARD relict of Thomas
deed of gift to children Thomas, George (200 acres
given me by my brother James KEMPE), Ann, Jacomin
and John. Wit: James NIMMO.

4DB287   6 May 1730: Audit of the estate of John
BOLITHO by Anthony WALKE Francis LAND, M. BOUSH.

4DB293   17 Mar 1729/30/9 May 1730: John GRIFFEN
- sons Henry, John, James and Charles; daughters Frances and Joyce. Ex: Henry and John. Wit: Henry HOLMES,
William HANCOCK.

4DB293   25 Oct 1729/6 May 1730: Esther POOLE -
daughter Mary SMITH, daughter Sarah THOROWGOOD, grandchildren George POOLE, Nathaniel NICKERSON, ____ GAS-
KING, Elizabeth RICHMOND and Elizabeth ISLAND. Ex:
sons Richard and William POOLE. Wit: John PORTER,
Mary KEELING, William POOLE.

4DB294   26 Apr 1730/3 Jun 1730: William NICHOLAS -
dons William, Josiah, Andrew, Glandwell, John and Isaac;
daughters Ann and Elizabeth. Ex: Andrew and John. Wit:
Thomas WHITEHURST, Samuel FENTRIS, Amos ____.

4DB299   13 Aug 172_/ 5 Aug 1730: James HAYNES -
sons John, Thomas, James and Erasmus, daughters Frances
and Margret BRUNT. Ex: Henry WOODHOUSE and son John.
Wit: Dinah SIMMONS, Henry WOODHOUSE, William KEELING.

4DB300   1 Nov 1727/5 Aug 1730:   Hillary MOSELEY - son Edward HACK MOSELEY, wife Hannah. Ex: wife. Wit: Elenor BROTT, Charles PORTLOCK, Blandinah SHIPLEY, Charles WILLIAMSON.

4DB305   - May 1726/1 Oct 1729:   Sampson TREVETHAN - wife Katherine, daughters Mary and Ann that I left behind in Virginia, William GWAVIS and Gregory TANNER of Penzance. Wit: George USALO, John RICHARDS, Andrew STONE.

4DB306   31 Aug 1730/4 Nov 1730:   James SMITH - brother John, son James, sister Amy BOND. Ex: brother John. Wit: John WHITEHURST, George SMYTH.

4DB311   23 Oct 1730/3 Dec 1730:   Ann CARTWRIGHT - son William, aon-in-law James COTTON, daughter Katherine, daughters Sarah KEELING, Frances CLAYDER and Ann KEELING, son John's children, son Thomas. Ex: sons William and Thomas. Wit: William POOLE, James GUARILL.

4DB312   8 Dec 172-/2 Dec 1730:   Anthony BARNS, Sr. - sons Daniel, John and Anthony; daughter Elizabeth CHAPPEL, son William. Ex: Anthony. Wit: John JAMES, Edward JAMES, Anthony BARNES.

4DB315   23 Dec 1730/6 Jan 1730/1:   George PURDY - sons William, Thomas, John and George; daughters Ursula and Elizabeth. Ex: son William and John IVY. Trustee: James NIMMO. Wit: William CARTWRIGHT, Thomas WILLIAMSON, James NIMMO.

4DB318   24 Jan 1730/1/3 Mar 1730/1:   Thomas ALBRITTON - wife Ann, son James. Ex: James. Wit: Solomon WHITE, William SIMMONS, Doyley LATTER.

4DB324   ---/19 Sep 1730:   Nathaniel HUTCHINGS - noncupative will - all to wife. Wit: Palmer MOSELEY, Richard DUDLEY.

4DB347   7 Jul 1731:   Dennis CREED and wife Martha only surviving child of John SIVILL Elder, dec. to Roger FOUNTAIN for 6 shillings 100 acres on the branches of Coratuck. Wit: M. BOUSH, John PILKINGTON.

4DB350   2 Dec 1729/5 May 1731:   Sarah HUTCHINGS - son s Nathaniel and John. Ex: Nathaniel. Wit: Frances CHAPPLIN, Josias TAINER.

4DB350   4 May 1731:   Elizabeth WHITE deed of gift to son James. Wit: William WHITE, Mary WHITE.

4DB355   11 May 1731/1 Sep 1731:   John MURRAY, Sr. - grandsons Caleb and John, David and Richard, wife Mary. Ex: wife and couzen William NICHOLSON. Wit: John NICKLIS, Jr., Richard BERRY, Ann SIMMONS·

4DB357   ---/1 Sep 1731:   Isaac TALBOT - sons Shadrack, Jesse and Jacob, wife Frances. Ex: John CONSOLBARE. Wit: Edward OWLD, George NORRIS.

4DB357   6·Sep 1731/2 Nov 1731:   Adam ACKIS - daughter Katherine, wife, cousen Adam son of by brother John. Wit: Ann COCKSIN, John SAUNDERS.

4DB382 4 Oct 1729/2 Mar 1731: William ASHLEY
- wife Mary, sister Elizabeth BENTLEY. Ex: wife.
Wit: John WISHARD, John GRIFFEN.

4DB389 1 Mar 1731/2: Edward MOSELEY deed of
gift to grandson Edward HACK MOSELEY. Wit: Christopher BURROUGH, Charles SAYER.

4DB397 26 Dec 1727/3 May 1732: William BONNEY -
sons Richard (manor plantation), William and John.
Ex: sons. Wit: Ursula BONNEY, Elizabeth HENLY, John
BONNEY.

4DB406 11 Feb 1731/7 Jun 1732: Daniel FRIZELL
- wife Elizabeth, sons Arthur, Daniel, Francis and
Edward; daughters Ruth and Elizabeth. Ex: wife.
Wit: William WEST, Renatus LAND, John GRIFFEN.

4DB408 29 Dec 1732/2 Aug 1743: William EASTER
- wife Mary, children Thomas, Frances, Mary, Jacomin,
John, William, Samuel, Abraham and James. Ex: wife.
Wit: John WISHARD, William PEED.

4DB412 6 Sep 1732: Joyce THELABALL deed of gift
to children Robert, Margret, Keziah and Mary - two
deceased children's share of their father's estate.
Wit: James NIMMO, Mary NIMMO.

4DB418 12 Jul 1732/6 Dec 1732: Lewis PURVINE -
son Thomas, sister Mary, daughter Sarah. Ex: son.
Wit: Francis THOROWGOOD, William BENSON, Amy THOROW-
GOOD.

4DB419 7 Feb 1732: Deposition of Christopher
BURROUGH (58), Patience BURROUGH (42) and Charles
SAYER (46) that they were well acquainted with Samp-
son TREVETHAN who married Ann widow of Argall THOROW-
GOOD and had two daughters Mary and Ann, and Mary
married Stephen WRIGHT.

4DB424 4 Nov 1732/3/7 Feb 1732: William WHITE-
HURST - sons Arthur and Odin, daughter Margret WRIGHT,
grandson Arthur LAMOUNT, daughter Bridget SNAILE, sons
Charles, Francis and Willis, wife Elizabeth. Ex:
wife. Wit: Ezra BROOKE, John WILBUR, Sr.

4DB432 7 Feb 1732: Audit of the estate of
Thomas EADINGS by James NIMMO, William POOLE.

4DB435 6 Mar 1732: Mathew ELLEGOOD eldest son
and heir of Mary PALLETT alias ELLEGOOD, dec. to
John ELLEGOOD of Norfolk Co. for 5 shillings 100
acres on Western Shore known as Timber Neck - same
land Mathew PALLETT left to his daughter Mary.
Wit: William POOLE, Charles SAYER, Jr.

4DB439 4 Jul 1733: John DAUGE deed of gift
to daughters Mary and Joan land in NC and VA.

4DB439 ---/4 Jul 1733: William CORBELL - son
Samuel, daughters Prudence, Mary and Elizabeth, wife
Elizabeth. Ex: wife. Wit: Solomon WHITE, Jr., John
BUCKNER, Josiah MORRIS.

4DB451   1 Aug 1733:   Thomas AXSTEAD deed of
gift to brother Henry of 120 acres - part of a
tract of 400 acres which was devised to him from
his grandfather's will.   Wit: Edward JAMES, Charles
KELLEY.

4DB453   8 May 1733/4 Aug 1733:   Henry HOLMES -
sons Henry, John and James; daughters Martha, Sarah,
Dinah, ____HANCOCK wife of William and Margret
GRIFFEN.   Ex: Henry.   Wit: James NIMMO.

4DB457   26 Apr 1733/1 Aug 1733:   John WARD -
sons Edward, John and William; wife Mary; daughters Sarah FRANKLIN, Mary and Abigall.   Ex: wife.
Wit: Elizabeth CORBELL, Christopher PHILPOTT, John
SMITH.

4DB457   13 Mar 1732/3/5 Sep 1733:   Sarah BOUSH
wife of Maximillian - son Lemuel land which formerly belonged to my brother Horatio WOODHOUSE, son
Maximillian, daughter Mary.   Ex: husband.   Wit:
John SAUNDERS, Mary SAUNDERS.

4DB459   - Jun 1733/5 Sep 1733:   John FENTRIS -
sons Moses, John, James, William and Lemuel; daughters Elizabeth, Mary, Ann and Sarah; wife Ann.   Ex:
wife.

4DB460   - Jul 1733/3 Oct 1733:   John JAMES,
Sr. - sons John, Gisborn and William; daughters
Mary, Amy, Susannah and Jane; wife Susannah.   Ex:
wife.   Wit: Andrew PEACOCK, Mary JAMES, Robert JAMES˙

4DB461   5 Sep 1733:   John CHESHIRE eldest son
and heir of Capt. Richard CHESHIRE and wife Sarah
one of daughters of Malachi THRUSTON, elder to
Richard POOLE for 80 lbs. 100 acres on the Western
Shore called Hall's Cabin.   Wit: Charles SAYER,
Amos MOSELEY.

4DB464   13 Jul 1733/3 Oct 1733:   Charles WIT-
SHARD - daughter Mary PARSONS, sons Willis (Becket's
Folly), Charles and John; daughters Elizabeth and
Sarah.   Ex: John.   Wit: John CAPS, Daniel FRANKLIN,
Dinah FRANKLIN.

4DB464   7 Nov 1733:   Division of property of
Thomas EWELL - sons James, Thomas and Solomon and
Robert BRAMBLE who married Mary daughter of Ewell.

4DB468   5 Feb 1732/3/5 Dec 1733:   George KEMPE -
son John, daughter Ann ACKIS, grandson John son of
James and Mary, son James.   Ex: James.   Wit: John
IVY, Arthur SAYER.

4DB469   23 Jan 1727/8/6 Feb 1733:   Peter FLOYD -
wife Elizabeth.   Ex: wife.   Wit: James ALBRITON,
John BONNEY, Ruth AIRS.

4DB469   6 Feb 1733:   Appraisal of estate of
Edward BRADSHAW by William KEELING, James LAMOUNT,
William COX.

4DB479   3 Dec 1733:   Job and Savil GASKING to
John HOPKINS for 6 shillings 100 acres in North
Woods - same land Alexander LILBURN left to daughters Joan and Amy. Wit: John CALDER, Francis SPRATT.
   4DB483   22 Aug 1732/6 Mar 1733:   George SMITH
son of William and Elizabeth - sister Elizabeth,
uncle John SMITH. Ex: uncle. Wit: Simon WHITE-
HURST, Henry SNAILE.
   4DB483   22 Mar 173-/6 Mar 1733:   William GUIS-
BORNE - son Amos, daughter Jane, wife Mary. Ex:
wife. Wit: ---- JAMES, Mary JAMES, Doyley LATTER.
   4DB483   18 Jan 1733/4/6 Feb 1733:   Richard
BONNEY - son Edward, daughter Sarah, brother John's
son William, wife Margret. Ex: wife. Wit: Peter
MALBONE, John BONNEY, Jr.
   4DB484   4 Dec 1733/6 Feb 1733:   John CANNON -
sons Thomas, John and Edward; daughters Mary, Elizabeth and Amy; wife Amey. Ex: wife. Wit: George
SIMMONS, Richard SIMMONS, James SPRATT.
   4DB484   9 Feb 1733/6 Mar 1733:   John JACKSON
- wife Susan, brother Richason, sister Kezia, sister
Barbra CORNICK. Ex: wife. Wit: Richard WICKER,
Eustis STRIPES.
   4DB485   9 Feb 1733/6 Mar 1733:   Richard MOY -
wife Mary, kinsman John RALY son of Thomas RALEY,
brother George. Ex: wife. Wit: John WICKINS,
Colemon ROE, Kitely ROE.
   4DB485   29 Nov 1733/2 Jan 1733:   Mary JAMES -
daughters Ruth and Elizabeth, sons Robert and Matthew. Ex: sons John and Edward. Wit: John BARNS,
Mary AYERS, Robert WARD.
   4DB486   2 Dec 1733/6 Feb 1733:   Ambros BURFOOT -
grandson Robert BURFOOT. Wit: Amy JOLLEY, William
COX, Abia COX.
   4DB497   15 Aug 1730/3 Apr 1734:   John HENLY -
sons Moses and John. Ex: wife and son John. Wit:
John GORNTO, Robert WARD, Mary GORNTO.
   4DB497   10 Jan 1733/4/3 Apr 1734:   Daniel
FRIZEL - brothers Arthur, Francis and Edward.
Ex: Arthur. Wit: John DAUGE, Elizabeth DAUGE.
   4DB499   11 Mar 1733/4/3 Apr 1734:   Phillip
WOODHOUSE - brother William. Ex: uncle Horatio
WOODHOUSE. Wit: John GORNTO, John BROWN, Francis
WOODHOUSE.
   4DB499   ---/12 Jan 1733/4:   Thomas DAULEY -
noncupative will - brothers Henry and William. Wit:
William DAULEY, Elizabeth DAULEY, Henry DAULEY.
   4DB500   ---/15 Apr 1734:   John DAUGE - wife
Elizabeth, sister Nowdina HENLEY, grandson John
WHITEHURST, brother William's son John, Francis
WOODHOUSE, all my brothers and sisters. Ex: Fran-
cis WOODHOUSE. Wit: John BONNEY, William DAUGE.

4DB500   3 Dec 1733/1 May 1734:   John OLIVER - sons Solomon, John and Joshua; wife Elizabeth; daughters Elizabeth and Abya. Ex: wife. Wit: Solomon WHITE, Mary PRICE, Thomas DAVIS.

4DB501   14 Feb 1733/4/1 May 1734:   James CUMBERFOOT - son John, wife and children. Ex: wife Margret. Wit: James WHITEHURST, William MACKCLALIN.

4DB501   1 May 1734:   James WILLIAMSON eldest son and heir of Charles WILLIAMSON to brother Charles for 10 shillings 584 acres on Knowel's Branch. Wit: Charles SAYER, James NIMMO.

4DB502   ---/1 May 1734:   Daniel FRANKLIN - noncupative will - wife Dyana FRALING. Wit: _____ FRANKLIN, Nathaniel FRANKLIN.

4DB503   10 Apr 1734/5 Jun 1734:   Edward LAMOUNT - sons Henry and Anthony, wife Elenor. Ex: wife. Wit: Henry LAMOUNT, John LAMOUNT, Charles MALBONE.

4DB506   3 Jun 1734/3 Jul 1734:   Hugh WHITEHURST - sons Caleb, Joshua, Jonathan and David; sister-in-law Elizabeth WHITEHURST. Ex: Moses PRESCOTT. Wit: Thomas WILES, Peter MORHOUSE, Henry WHITEHURST.

4DB507   16 Feb 1733/4/5 Jun 1734:   John SAUNDERS - wife Mary, son Jonathan, daughters Mary and Margret, unborn child. Ex: wife and Arthur SAWER. Wit: John GUY, Henry MILLER.

4DB507   16 Apr 1734/3 Jul 1734:   Edward CANNON - wife Elizabeth, son John. Ex: wife. Wit: Benony SMYTH, John CAPPS.

4DB507   15 Jun 1734/3 Jul 1734:   Elizabeth WHITEHURST - daughter Mary, sons Gideon and Enuch. Ex: Gideon. Wit: James CARROWAY, Richard WHITEHURST.

4DB517   3 May 1734/7 Aug 1734:   William LESTER - son Willis, wife Elizabeth. Ex: wife. Wit: John RUSSELL, William OAKHAM.

4DB517   9 Aug 1734/4 Sep 1734:   William ACKISS - brother John, sons Francis and Nathaniel, daughters Sarah and Frances. Ex: William CARTWRIGHT. Wit: Francis ACKIS, William POOLE.

4DB518   28 Mar 1733/7 Aug 1734:   Katherine ACKIS - son William, William's daughter Katherine, granddaughter Mary EDWARDS, Elizabeth daughter of son Francis. Ex: son Francis. Wit: Anthony WALKE, John KEMPE, Francis ACKISS.

4DB518   12 Mar 1731/4 Sep 1734:   Lemuel IVY, mariner being bound out of country - brother John. Wit: Thomas BINGHAM, Lemuell PORTLOCK.

4DB525   22 Oct 1734:   Anthony MOSELEY deed of gift to daughter Abigall. Wit: Henry MOORE, Charles SMYTH.

4DB526   6 Dec 1732:   Division of land of Cason
MOORE elder - five children William, Cason, Sarah
who married James CONDON, Frances who married Smith
SHEPHERD, Elizabeth who married Matthew PALLETT -
by Jacob ELLEGOOD, Thomas HAYNES, William BENSON.

4DB526   6 Nov 1734:   Margret BONNEY deed of
gift to son Edward and daughter Sarah.   Wit: James
WHITEHUS, James CASON.

4DB527   2 Oct 1734/6 Nov 1734:   Naomy MACKEEL -
son-in-law Jacob MACLOUD, son Hezekiah MACLOUD,
daughter Mary CUPER, daughter Sarah CUPER.   Ex:
Jacob MACLOUD.   Wit: John GRIFFEN, Adam THOROWGOOD.

4DB527   12 Oct 1734./1 Jan 1734/5:   Owen JONES
- sons Robert and Owan.   Wit: John ELKS, Andrew
BRAND.

4DB527   28 Jul 1734/6 Nov 1734:   Thomas THRILL-
WIND - wife Blandinah.   Ex: wife.   Wit: Thomas TYSON,
Frances ROBINSON.

4DB532   5 Feb 1734:   Richard LESTER to son
Richard gift of 135 acres on North branches of
Coratuck.   Wit: William OAKHAM, Henry CAPPS,
Andrew PEACOCK.

4DB534   5 Mar 1734:   Appraisement of the estate
of Hardis LAMOND.

4DB540   26 Mar 1735:   Inventory of the estate
of David HOLT sworn to by Mary HOLT and John HOLT.

4DB541   5 Jun 1734:   Depositions of Edward
MOSELEY (73), John MOSELEY (64), and Margret SAYER
(59) that Thomas WALKE, merchant who came from
Barbados married Mary daughter of Anthony LAWSON
and had three children - Thomas, Anthony and Mary.

4DB548   7 May 1735:   Thomas WILES, Sr. deed
of gift to children Thomas, Jr., Lemuel, Samuel,
Mary, Elizabeth, and Sarah Ann VEALE.   Wit: Anthony
WALKE, James NIMMO.

4DB549   17 Feb 1723/4/7 May 1735:   Edward
WOOD - sons William, Mark and John, wife.   Ex:
William.   Wit: Thomas NASH, Sr., Ann NASH, Solo-
mon NASH.

4DB549   18 Mar 1731/2/7 May 1735:   Thomas
LAWSON - wife Frances, three sons Anthony, Thomas,
and Charles.   Ex: wife and father-in-law Charles
SAYER.

4DB550   7 May 1735:   Inventory of the estate
of John WARD sworn to by Mary WARD and Edward WARD.

DEED BOOK FIVE

5DB3   3 Feb 1734/4 Jun 1735:   Thomas BERRY -
Richard COATS, sons John, George and Thomas. Ex:
Thomas. Wit: John WHITEHEAD, Uestes STRIPES.
    5DB3   ---/4 Jun 1735: Dennis CREEDS - son
John, wife Martha. Wit: Joseph COOPER, Richard
SMITH.
    5DB7   ---/26 May 1735:   William SHIPP - sons
John and Willis, John HOPKINS, Jr., daughters Ann,
Sarah SIMSON, Elizabeth CANNON, Cattern NICHOLS;
seven younger children, wife Mary. Ex: wife and
Steven PEW. Wit: Luke MOSELEY, Steven PEW.
    5DB15   11 May 1735/6 Aug 1735:   David HARPER -
sons David and William, wife Ann. Ex: James NIMMO
and John HARPER. Wit: James THELABELL, Mary HARPER.
    5DB18   27 Sep 1734/3 Feb 1734:   Solomon WHITE -
daughters Elizabeth, Mary and Isabell, son Solomon.
Ex: Capt. Robert VAUGHAN. Wit: Patrick WHITE, Sr.,
Patrick WHITE, Jr., Providence SIMONS.
    5DB18   3 Sep 1735: Appraisal of the estate
of Thomas FRENCH by John WHITEHURST, John KNOWIS.
    5DB20   28 Jul 1735/3 Sep 1735:   Elizabeth
CANNON - son John, Elizabeth MOORE daughter of
Henry MOORE, Jr., brother-in-law Henry MOORE.
Ex: Henry MOORE. Wit: T. KEEL, Sarah MOORE, Ed-
ward HOWARD.
    5DB20   22 Oct 1734/3 Sep 1735:   Mark WOOD -
wife Sara, sons William, Mark and Solomon, daugh-
ter Abbe SALTER, granddaughters Elizabeth and Sary
SALTER. Ex: wife. Wit: Moses FENTRIS, Christopher
SALTER, James FENTRIS.
    5DB22   26 Aug 1735:   John WISHARD and wife
Frances and James KEMPE and wife Mary daughters
of George HANCOCK divide 500 acres known as Wolves
Nick which HANCOCK lived on. Wit: James NIMMO,
James MOORE.
    5DB29   29 Sep 1735:   Amy CONNER deed of gift
to children Thomas CANNON, Edward CANNON, Elizabeth CANNON and Amy CANNON.
    5DB34   18 Aug 1735/5 Nov 1735:   Baron MORSE -
land to be sold by brother John and John BONNEY and
equally divided between sons Thomas and Jonathan.
Ex: John MOORE and John BONNEY. Wit: Thomas WARD,
John HENLEY, John GRIFFEN.

5DB37   26 Aug 1735/3 Dec 1735:   Elizabeth
EATON - friend John DYER my part of land my father
Michael lived on, sister Ann wife of Matthew CAPPS.
Ex: John DYER.   Wit: William DYER, James MOORE,
Andrew PEACOCK.

5DB43   1 Oct 1735:   Audit of the estate of
John DOREY by Thomas WISHART, James HUNTER.

5DB44   4 Dec 1735/3 Mar 1735:   Abraham MILL -
Thomas WISHART.   Ex: Thomas WISHART.   Wit: Lewis
CONNER, Arthur SAYER.

5DB48   27 Oct 1735/8 Jan 1735:   Anthony MOSE-
LEY - wife Frances, daughters Ann and Mary.   Ex:
wife.   Wit: Palmer MOSELEY, Edward PEARY.

5DB49   5 Nov 1735/8 Jan 1735:   Robert RICH-
MOND - sons Robert, William and Anthony, William
BENSON, daughters Elizabeth and Mary.   Ex: brother
William.   Wit: Thomas HAYNES, Erasmus HAYNES,
Lancaster LOVETT.

5DB53   27 Aug 1735/4 Feb 1735:   David MCCLE-
NAHAN - mother Elizabeth, cousens Nathaniel, Ann,
David and Nathaniel MCCLENAHAN, Elizabeth MCCLE-
NAHAN ROBINSON daughter of Mary ROBINSON.   Ex:
mother.   Wit: John FITTZ, Edward DENBY, Emperor
MOSELEY.

5DB54   10 Jan 1730/1/4 Feb 1735:   George
HANCOCK - sisters Frances and Mary, uncle Wil-
liam HANCOCK.   Ex: uncle.   Wit: Henry GRIFEN,
John WISHARD.

5DB58   7 Apr 1736:   Susannah CHESHIRE deed
of gift to children John THOROWGOOD, Elizabeth
CHESHIRE, Pembrook WRIGHT.   Wit: Charles SAYER,
Arthur SAYER.

5DB59   6 Mar 1735/6/7 Apr 1736:   Col Edward
MOSELEY - wife Isabella, grandson Edward HACK
MOSELEY, cousen Anthony MOSELEY mariner, John
son of cousen Anthony, Edward son of Capt. Fran-
cis MOSELEY, Stringer MOSELEY son of William,
Richard MOSELEY.   Ex: Capt. Francis MOSELEY, Charles
MALBONE and Arthur SAYER.   Wit: William HAPPER,
Anthony WALKE, Blandinah MOSELEY, Anthony MOSELEY.

5DB62   4 Aug 1736:   Inventory of the estate
of Thomas CREED given by Jane CREED.

5DB64   26 Dec 1735/5 Mar 1735:   Mary WISHARD -
daughters Dinah, Mary WILLIAMS, Frances COLLINS;
granddaughter Mary BRAY, son Jacob JOHNSON WISHARD.
Ex: son John WISHARD.   Wit: John JEAMASON, George
COLLINS.

5DB68   29 Mar 1736/5 May 1736:   John DAULEY -
son William (plantation in Muddy Creek and land
called Bevils), daughters Mary, Ann and Sary, wife
Mary.   Ex: wife.   Wit: Henry DAULEY, Martha CAPPS,
Ann CAPPS.

5DB71   1 Apr 1736/5 May 1736:   Francis LAND -
wife Margret, son Francis THOROWGOOD LAND, daughters Mary and Margret. Ex: wife. Wit: Job GAS-
KING, Abigail KEELING, Jacob ELLEGOOD.

5DB76   26 Dec 1735/5 May 1736: Ann TREVETHAN,
Jr. - cousins James TENNANT, Elizabeth TENNANT, and
Mary Ann THOROWGOOD, mother Ann TREVETHAN. Ex:
mother and Anthony MOSELEY. Wit: Christopher BUR-
ROUGH, Robert THOROWGOOD.

5DB79   3 May 1736:   Audit of the estate of
Leonard TURTAIN by William DYER and Andrew PEACOCK.

5DB79   5 May 1736:   Mary BROWN and Ann SPANN
of Norfolk Co. to Solomon WALLICE for 10 lbs. 100
acres near Pungo Chappel which fell to them by the
death of their father who purchased it from Peter
MALBONE. Wit: Coleman ROE, Sofia FENTRESS, Mary
ROE.

5DB82   24 Mar 1735/6/2 Jun 1736:   Thomas PURDY
- cosen William PURDY son of my brother William
PURDY, cosen Thomas PURDY, brother William. Wit:
William WEST, Thomas CREED.

5DB97   22 Nov 1735/6 Oct 1736:   Thomas MOOR -
sons Thomas, James, Henry, Moses, Arthur and William;
daughters Ann and Susannah; wife Margret. Ex: son
James and cousin John WHITEHURST.

5DB98   29 Nov 1735/5 Jan 1736:   Matthew KILLEY
- wife Mary. Ex: wife. Wit: Job GASKING, Charles
MALBONE.

5DB144   2 Jan 1736/7:   Charles MALBONE deed
of gift to son and daughter-in-law Francis THOROW-
GOOD LAND and Margret LAND. Wit: Jacob ELLEGOOD,
Francis MOSELEY.

5DB142   25 Sep 1729/1 Feb 1736:   Agreement
between Eve ETHERIDGE, Moses BALL and Elizabeth
his wife and Richard STANDLY and Mary his wife
heirs of John MURRAY - division of land. Wit:
Mary MURRAY, James TIMBERLAKE.

5DB144   12 Jul 1736/5 Jan 1736:   John HOPKINS
- wife Perscila, son Joshua, grandson John HOPKINS,
heirs of son Jehosaphat, grandson John STONE, granddaughter Dinah HOPKINS, son John, daughter Keziah,
daughter Mary FENTRIS, daughter Sarah, daughter
Elizabeth STONE, daughter Katherine. Ex: wife and
son-in-law John FENTRIS. Wit: John KEMPE, Thomas
WILLIAMSON, Carroway WHITEHURST.

5DB156   9 Sep 1736/2 Jun 1736:   John SALMON -
sons Richard and John, granddaughter Elizabeth
daughter of Richard, wife Geen, daughter Elizabeth
FENTRIS, daughter Dinah SUGG, granddaughters Eli-
zabeth and Sarah daughters of son John, grandson
John son of son William, granddaughters Mary and
Eliza daughters of son Anthony. Ex: wife and son
Richard. Wit: John WHITEHURST, Luis BECKER.

5DB164   2 Mar 1736: Appraisal of the estate
of James CUMBERFOOT by John JAMES, John HENLEY and
Peter MALBONE.

5DB165   15 Mar 1735/6/5 Jan 1736: William
HANCOCK - wife Mary, whild wife goes with, daugh-
ter Susannah, cousen Arthur MOSELEY, if daughter
dies her share to Richard, William and Blandina
MOSELEY, godson Henry GRIFFEN. Ex: wife. Wit:
James NIMMO, Henry HOLMES.

5DB166   6 Sep 1736/2 Feb 1736: John MALBONE -
wife Margret, son Solomon, daughters Frances and
Sarah, land at Long Island to be sold and money
divided between sons Reodolphus and Shadrack,
daughters Dinah DAUGE and Elizabeth DAULEY,
granddaughter Aleix MALBON. Ex: wife. Wit:
William DAULEY, William CARREL, James ALBRITTON.

5DB167   24 Apr 1736/2 Mar 1736: Major Henry
SPRATT - sons Francis, Thorowgood and Adam. Ex:
James NIMMO and son Thorowgood. Wit: James SPRATT,
Francis ROBINSON, Henry HOLMES.

5DB168   12 Jan 1736/7/2 Feb 1736: William
WISHART - kinsman Francis WISHART, cousen Thomas
WISHART. Ex: Thomas. Wit: James HUNTER, Hugh
BARLOW.

5DB171   2 Mar 1736/7/4 May 1737: Alexander
HARVEY - sons George, Thomas and John, daughter
Ann. Ex: son George and cozen John HARVEY. Wit:
William POOLE, John GRIFIN.

5DB182   2 Mar 1736/7: John WHITEHURST who
married a daughter of Robert MURDEN as trustee
for orphans receives estate from John KNOWIS who
married Sarah relict of MURDEN. Wit: John LOVETT,
William POOLE, Thomas HAYNES.

5DB209   7 Sep 1737: Appraisal of the estate
of Henry PHILPOTT.

5DB218   23 Jul 1737/3 Aug 1737: Jane SALMON
deed of gift to son John, Elizabeth HOPKINS daughter of John, goddaughter Mary STONE daughter of
John STONE. Wit: William STONE, William SHIPP.

5DB234   20 Aug 1737: Audit of John ASHBY
by Andrew PEACOCK, John BONNEY and Peter MALBONE.

5DB233   7 Oct 1729/4 Jan 1737: Mary WHITE-
HURST - daughter Elizabeth MOSELEY. Ex: daughter.
Wit: John SAUNDERS, William POOLE.

5DB234   29 Aug 1737/1 Feb 1737: Thomas CASON
- sons James and Thomas; daughters Margritt WIL-
LIAMSON, Sarah, Mary, Elizabeth, Jane, Ann and
Ruth; wife Margritt. Ex: Thomas. Wit: Elizabeth
DAUGE. Frances FRIZELL, William WEST.

5DB236   5 Apr 1738: Inventory of the estate
of Thomas PURVINE by Isaac WHITE.

5DB236   9 Nov 1737/1 May 1737:   Christopher
BURROUGH - sons Benony and Anthony, daughter Flo-
rence WHITEHURST, daughter Elizabeth, wife Patience.
Ex: wife. Wit: Charles SAYER, Nathaniel NEWTON.

5DB238   28 Mar 1738:   James HARRISON deed of
gift to children Mary, Thomas, John, Ann and Elizabeth. Wit: Jacob ELLEGOOD, Ann ELLEGOOD.

5DB241   18 Feb 1737/5 Apr 1738:   Edward OULD
- brother Thomas, son Arthur, daughters Rebecker,
Venues and Aticha, wife Venues. Ex: wife. Wit:
John ELLKS, John ROSE, Owen JONES.

5DB243   30 Jan 1737/7 Jun 1738:   John BRINSON
- sons Mathew, Adam and Henry (Possum Quarter),
daughter Susan, wife Elizabeth. Ex: wife. Wit:
John GRIFIN, John JAMES.

5DB248   17 Feb 1737/8/3 May 1738:   Henry
SNAILE - daughter Elizabeth COTTON, sons John,
Henry and Simon, daughters Sarah, Frances and
Mary, estate due me from their grandfather Wil-
liam WHITEHURST, wife Bridget. Ex: wife. Wit:
John WHITEHURST, Simon WHITEHURST.

5DB266   15 Feb 1737/8/2 Aug 1738:   Mary MC-
GRAVEY - granddaughter Mary Ann DALE. Ex: son-in-
law Paul DALE. Wit: Eliza DALE, William BENSON,
William COX.

5DB267   5 Jul 1738:   Ann TREVETHAN (60), Abigal CAWSON (50) alias WHIDDON and Abigail MOSELEY
(43) make oath that Abigal was married to Mr.
Jonas CAWSON, dec. and had children Keziah, Christopher, Argal, Ann, Abigall, Janet and Jonas before his death in 1726 and Keziah died in 1732.

5DB280   --Apr 1738/6 Jul 1738:   John LOVETT -
wife Mary, sons John and Lancaster, daughters
Amy THOROWGOOD, Isabell and Betty. REST MUTI-
LATED.

5DB355   23 Jan 1737/8/4 Apr 1739:   Joseph
HARMON - son Joseph, wife Elizabeth, BADLY
MUTILATED.

5DB282   6 Jun 1738/2 Aug 1738:   Richard POOLE
- son Alexander, wife Ann, daughters Elizabeth and
Sarah. Ex: James KEMPE and Thomas HAYNES.
MUTILATED.

5DB282   26 Jun 1738:   William POOLE - son
George, wife , daughter Martha. Wit: Job GASKING
Sarah THOROWGOOD. MUTILATED.

5DB382   22 Jul 1738:   Audit of the estate of
John BRIER by Thomas LAMOUNT, James LAMOUNT and
William COX.

5DB312   4 Aug --/7 Feb 1738:   Richard COOK -
daughters Hannah and Mary, wife Ann. Ex: wife.
Wit: William KEELING, William COTTON.

5DB311   4 Dec 1738/3 Jan 1738:   Aaron FENTRIS
son George, daughters Oliff and Betty, Franson wife
to _____ BARRINGTON. Ex: daughter Oliff. Wit:
William COLLINS, Dorcas GWIN.

5DB311   7 Feb 1738:   Moses FENTRIS, Sr. deed
of gift to children Moses, Aaron, Lemuel, Hezekiah
and Abiah SALMONS, wife Martha   MUTILATED.

5DB383   1 Aug 1739:   Andrew NICHOLAS to John
NICHOLAS, mariner to 5 shillings 100 acres on the
South side of the Eastern Branch which their fa-
ther bought of John BOLITHOE. Wit: James KEMPE,
John WISHARD, Peter JOHNSON.

5DB401   13 Jul 1739/3 Oct 1739:   John GUIS-
BORN - sons John, James, Thomas, Edward and Wil-
liam; wife Elizabeth; daughters Isabella and Jane
LANE. Ex: wife and son John. Wit: Robert REED,
Edward GISBORNE, Thomas SUGGS, John ROGERS.

5DB403   14 Sep 1739:   John WARD to brother
Edward WARD for 5 shillings 75 acres known as Pungar Plantation near Pungar Chappel being half of
a plantation my father John left my brother William.
Wit: Benjamin CUMMINGS, Edmond DOD, John ROGERS.

5DB411   24 Aug 1739:   George WEBLIN, eldest
son and heir of Elizabeth WEBLIN, dec. and Edward
SHARP and wife Dinah (Elizabeth and Dinah are
daughters of John GOODACRE, dec. and coheirs of
William GOODAKER who died without heirs) to Col.
Anthony WALKE for 5 shillings 60 acres near ye ᴑ
brick church and old courthouse. Wit: James KEMPE,
John KEMPE, William NIMMO, Edward DENBY, Thomas
HAYNES, Nathaniel LILBURN.

5DB416   7 Jul 1739/7 Nov 1739:   James LAMOUNT
- sons James and Edward, brother Thomas, daughter
Sarah, wife Mary. Wit: John LAMOUNT, Lemuel COR-
NICK.

4DB419   23 Sep 1739/7 Nov 1739:   John JONES -
son Edward, wife Ann, son John, (Ann SPANN who is
known as John's wife shall not inherit his share)
sons Simon and Henry, daughter Ann MESSER, daughter
Sarah MOORE. Ex: son Edward. Wit: Adam TOOLY,
Israel SLATTER, William WOOD, John ROGERS.

5DB421   28 Jan 1739/7 Nov 1739:   Simon HANCOCK
- wife Ann, son William, daughter Mary MALBONE,
grandchildren Joshua HANCOCK, John BIDDLE, William
BIDDLE, Mary BIDDLE, Elizabeth BIDDLE, daughter
Elizabeth BOUSH, grandchildren Elizabeth BOUSH,
Maximillian BOUSH, John HANCOCK and Sarah HANCOCK.
Ex: wife and William. Wit: Thomas FAZACKERLEY,
William HORSLEY, Edward DENBY, Peter JOHNSON.

5DB424   23 Sep 1739/5 Dec 1739:   Lawrence
BRINDLE - John BONNEY, daughters Mary and Elizabeth. Ex: daughters. Wit: William CARRILL, William SENECA.

5DB433   26 Nov 1739/2 Jan 1739:   George SMYTH
wife West, son Tully ROBINSON SMYTH.   Ex: wife.
Wit: Charles SMYTH, Benony SMYTH, Mary ROBINSON,
Ann HANCOCK.

5DB450   17 Oct 1739/2 Apr 1740:   William SIM-
MONS - sons Uriah, John and William; daughter Mary;
wife Ann; wife's daughter Betty HARBERT.   Ex: wife.
Wit: Southwood SIMMONS, John ROGERS, Adam TOOLY.

5DB451   8 Mar 1739/2 Apr 1740:   Isabelle MOSE-
LEY - cousins James IVES, Robert BURGESS, Robert
HODGES, Ann FAZACKERLY, Emanuel BURGESS, Thomas
BURGESS, Mary HODGES; sister Elizabeth HODGES,
Mary MERRIS, cousin Richard HODGES, Mr. Edward
HACK MOSELEY.   Ex: Robert BURGESS AND Robert
HODGES.   Wit: Thomas WALKE, John BIDDLE.

5DB453   9 Jan 1737/8/2 Apr 1740:   Thomas WHITE-
HURST - daughter Pation GODFREY, sons Smyth, Lemuel,
Thomas and James (land at Three Runs); daughters
Sarah and Martha; wife; three youngest sons Peter,
Christopher and William.   Ex: wife and Lemuel.
Wit: Thomas WILES, George SHIRLEY, Richard BERRY.

5DB466   2 Apr 1740:   Audit of the estate of
Joseph GWIN by Arthur SAYER, William PARSONS,
Charles SMYTH.

5DB475   21 Apr 1740/7 May 1740:   William RICH-
MOND - cousen William RICHMOND, cousen Anthony
RICHMOND.   Ex: Henry WOODHOUSE and William KEELING.
Wit: Adam KEELING, Robert RICHMOND.

5DB476   21 Jan 1739/7 May 1740:   Edward JONES
of Blackwater - brother Simon (plantation that my
father John left me), brother John, sister Anne
MESSER, sister Sarah MOORE, brother Henry.   Ex:
brothers Henry and Simon.   Wit: Letitia BUCK,
Joseph DOBBS, John ROGERS.

5DB479   20 Mar 1739/40/4 Jun 1740:   John WIL--
LOUGHBY - son Thomas, daughter Elizabeth, wife
Elizabeth.   Ex: wife.   Wit: Elizabeth CUMMINGS,
William WILLOUGHBY, John ROGERS.

5DB480   22 Nov 1739/4 Jun 1740:   Edward PERRY -
sister (estate left by father Joseph), friend James
WILLIAMSON.   Ex: James WILLIAMSON.   Wit: Caleb NASH,
William BARRINGTON.

5DB480   16 Jul 1737/4 Jun 1740:   Jane CREED -
Thomas CREED son of William.   Ex: Thomas.   Wit:
James COTTON, Sarah CASON, Henry SNAILE.

5DB489   15 Apr 1739/2 Jul 1740:   John MOSE-
LEY - sons Francis and Anthony, daughter Elen wife
of Abia COX, daughter Mary wife of Capt. Henry MOORE.
Ex: sons and son-in-law Henry MOORE.   Wit: Francis
MOSELEY, Robert WHITEHURST.

5DB492   6 Aug 1740:   Appraisal of the estate
of Edmond DAVIS by John WHITEHURST, Francis LAND,
John SMYTH.

5DB501   20 Aug 1733/1 Oct 1740:   Grace SHER-
WOOD - sons John, James and Richard. Ex: John.
Wit: John WILBUR, John BERRY, John BURGESS.

5DB501   1 Oct 1740:   Inventory of the estate
of James BROCK dec. 20 Sep 1740 by John HARPER,
Anthony MOSELEY, Bartholomew WILLIAMSON, John
THOROWGOOD.

5DB502   29 Sep 1740:   Charles WHITEHURST to
brother Odeon 150 acres. Wit: Thomas LANGLEY,
Arthur WHITEHURST, Patrick MURPHY.

5DB504   18 Aug 1740/5 Nov 1740:   Charles SAYER
- wife Margret, son Arthur, daughter Frances BOUSH,
daughter Elizabeth NEWTON, grandchildren Mary BOUSH,
Thomas LAWSON, Charles LAWSON, Anne NEWTON, Anthony
LAWSON, Arthur BOUSH and Frances SAYER, son-in-law
Nathaniel NEWTON. Ex: son Arthur. Wit: Thomas
HUNTER, Patience BURROUGH, Mary SAUNDERS.

5DB526   3 Dec 1740:   Mary WILLIAMS relict of
Edward BRAY and Elizabeth and Mary BRAY daughters
of Edward BRAY to Tully ROBINSON SMYTH for 5 shillings 200 acres on Broad Creek. Wit: Matthew ELLE-
GOOD, William MOYE, John BURFOOT.

5DB532   12 Dec 1740/7 Jan 1740:   Henry COLLINS
- sons John, George and Lemuel, wife Anne, daughter
Sarah. Ex: wife. Wit: Mary GRANT, Solomon BOUSH,
John JAMESON.

5DB533   12 Dec 1740:   Roger WILLIAMSON eldest
son and heir of Richard WILLIAMSON to brother John
60 acres which father Richard wanted him to have.
Wit: John KEMPE, John THOROWGOOD, Peter MALBONE,
Edward BONNEY.

5DB534   14 Aug 1734/7 Jan 1740:   John JAMES -
sons William, Edward and Jonathan, daughter Mary,
wife Elizabeth. Ex: wife. Wit: John BUTLER, Henry
JAMES, Richard BRINSON.

5DB535   30 Jun 1740/7 Jan 1740:   Thomas COR-
NISH of Blackwater - sons William, Thomas and Elias
(land given by father Thomas), daughter Elizabeth,
wife Ales, brother Elias. Wit: John KNOWIS, Owen
JONES, John ROGERS.

DEED BOOK SIX

6DB1   12 Apr 1739: Thomas BOLITHOE acknow-
ledges receipt of full payments of all sums due the
estate of his uncle John BOLITHOE from John NICHOLAS
who intermarried with Yates admnx of John BOLITHOE,
dec. Wit: James KEMPE, William NIMMO.
6DB1   13 Dec 1740: Roger WILLIAMSON son and heir
of Richard WILLIAMSON to Anthony WALKE for 8 lbs. 50
acres left to brother John. Wit: John KEMPE, Tully
WILLIAMSON, William HAPPER, Morrice SULLIVAN.
6DB8   4 Mar 1740: Audit of Darby MCCARTY by
Andrew PEACOCK, John BONNEY, Sr. John GORNTO.
6DB9   4 Jan 1740/4 Mar 1741: William ROBINSON-
son William, son Tully (Little Island), divide Porter's Ridge equally; sisters Sarah SMITH, Mary ROBIN-
SON and Annie HANCOCK. Ex: sons and sister Mary.
Overseers: Alexander CAMPBELL, Edward HACK MOSELEY,
John NICHOLAS and William NIMMO. Wit: William HAN-
COCK, Emperor MOSELEY, William NIMMO, Nathaniel MC-
CLENAHAN.
6DB15   6 Dec 1740/1 Apr 1741: Charles MALBONE -
sons James, William and Charles, wife Margaret. Ex:
wife. Wit: Mary THOROWGOOD, Jacob ELLEGOOD.
6DB15   ---/1 Apr 1741: John SHIPP - sons William
and Francis, daughters Katharine EDWARDS and Mary
ALLEN, cousin Adam ACKISS, wife Ann. Ex: wife and
son William. Wit: Simon WHITEHURST, James SMYTH.
6DB16   13 Feb 1740/1 Apr 1741: Francis THOROW-
GOOD - wife Amy, eldest son John, hers and my children. Ex: wife. Wit: John CONNYER, Joel SIMMONS,
John DUNNOCK.
6DB17   1 Apr 1740: Cason BUSKY and wife Mary
(only daughter of John and Elizabeth CANNON and one
of two sisters (?) and coheirs of Edward LAND, Jr.)
to Anthony WALKE for 5 shillings 670 acres wheron
Mary's grandfather Edward LAND lived. Wit: Jacob
ELLEGOOD, Edward HACK MOSELEY, John HUTCHINGS.
6DB19   1 Apr 1741: Benjamin DAUGE of Curratuck
in NC to John FENTRESS, Jr. for 5 shillings 130 acres
- same land James DAUGE gave in his will to his son
Richard. Wit: Anthony WALKE, John KEMPE, John FEN-
TRESS, Michael FENTRESS.

6DB35   7 May 1741:   Anthony WALKE, Jr. son and
heir of Col. Thomas WALKE to brother Thomas WALKE
for 5 shillings 300 acres. Wit: James NIMMO, James
WILLIAMSON, George WEBLIN, Bartholomew WILLIAMSON.

6DB37   6 May 1741:   James WISHART of Accomack
Co to brother Thomas WISHART for 5 shillings 260
acres in Little Creek. Wit: William NIMMO, James
BANNISTER, Robert BURROUGH.

6DB42   7 May 1741:   Richard DUDLEY to sons
Richard and John deed of gift of 190 acres on Ben-
nett's Creek. Wit: Nathaniel NEWTON, William NIMMO,
John NICHOLAS.

6DB44   6 May 1741:   Catharine LILBURN daughter
of William LILBURN, dec. obtainedan order against
John CONNYER who married the widow of the dec. -
now releases order. Wit: Ezra BROOKE, Francis
SPRATT.

6DB45   18 Jan 1741/6 May 1741:   John SMYTH -
sons James (land in Creed's Neck), John and William,
wife Mary. Ex: wife and Simon WHITEHURST and son
James. Wit: Thomas LANGLEY, Martha BOND.

6DB49   27 Aug 1740/3 Jun 1741:   Jacob LANGLEY -
brothers William, Nathan, James and Abraham; George
IVY who married my sister Elizabeth, sister Margaret
JOHNSON, John WISHARD who married my sister Joyce,
cousin William IVY, cousin Jacob son of my brother
William, cousin Joseph LANGLEY, brother Jeremiah.
Ex: Jeremiah. Wit: Matthew ELLEGOOD, Joel CORNICK,
Charles MALBONE.

6DB51   1 Jul 1741:   Erasmus HAYNES and Anthony
LEGATT (son and heir of Amy LEGATT, dec. wife of
Alexander LEGATT) to Col. Anthony WALKE for 5 shil-
lings 48 acres. Wit: Arthur SAYER, Thomas HAYNES.

6DB57   5 Aug 1741:   John MCNEIL and wife Elizabeth (daughter of John SALMON grandson of John SALMON
who gave his son John grandfather of said Elizabeth)
for 5 lbs. 240 acres to Richard CORBITT. Wit: Anthony WALKE, Nathaniel NEWTON, John KEMP, William
NIMMO.

6DB59   5 Aug 1741:   Thomas LOVE and wife Sarah
(one of two daughters and coheirs of John SALMON
who was grandson and heir of John SALMON Elder) to
Richard CORBETT for 5 lbs. 240 acres. Wit: Anthony
WALKE, Nathaniel NEWTON, John KEMP, William NIMMO.

6DB56   19 Jul 1740/5 Aug 1741:   James TENANT,
mariner - godson John THOROWGOOD, Jr., grandmother
Ann TREVETHAN, cousin Mary Ann THOROWGOOD, brother-
in-law Roderick CONNER, brother Samuel, sister Elizabeth. Ex: James NIMMO and William NIMMO, Sr. Wit:
Wit: Charles SMYTH, Edward DENBY, Emperor MOSELEY.

6DB89   19 Oct 1741/4 Nov 1741:   Ezra BROOK -
wife Sarah. Ex: Rev Henry BARLOW, Patrick BROOKE,
Anthony MOSELEY.

6DB98   2 Oct 1741:   John JAMESON deed of gift
to son Henry land and marshes known as Cases Entry
by the Ragged Islands. Wit: James NIMMO, James
CONDON.

6DB99   2 Nov 1741/2 Oct 1741:   John NORRIS -
sons John, Charles and George; daughters Sarah and
Ann, wife Ann. Ex: William CARTWRIGHT and James
CARROWAY. Wit: Arthur SAYER, Thomas CARTWRIGHT.

6DB100   6 Jan 1741:   Thorowgood SPRATT to James
MOORE 100 acres in Nanny's Creek purchased from Adam
SPRATT who heired it from father Henry. Wit: William
NIMMO, John PUGH, Gabriel CLAYTON.

6DB101   ---/6 Jan 1741:   Henry JAMES - sons
Henry and Robert, wife Bridget, brothers Matthew
and John. Ex: wife. Wit: Matthew BRINSON, John
DEARMORE.

6DB101   31 Dec 1741/3 Feb 1741:   James THELA-
BALL - mother Abigail MOSELEY, brothers Lewis, Nath-
aniel, Thomas and Lemuel. Ex: father-in-law Anthony
MOSELEY and brother Thomas. Wit: Elizabeth NICHOL-
SON, Sarah JONES, William MOYE.

6DB105   26 Feb 1741/2/3 Mar 1741:   Elizabeth
WOODHOUSE - son William WHITE, daughters Elizabeth
KEY and Mary SPARROW, daughter Kezia WHITE, son
James WHITE, daughter Sarah WHITE. Ex: son-in-law
Peter SPARROW. Wit: William KEELING, Sr., William
KEELING, Jr.

6DB118   7 Apr 1742:   John SHIPP deed of gift
to kinsmen William and Francis SHIP 100 acres of
swampland. Wit: John STONE, Titus CHERRY.

6DB118   16 Dec 1741/7 Apr 1742:   John GRIFFEN -
wife Sarah, sons George, James and John. Ex: wife.
Wit: James NIMMO, Thomas BANKS.

6DB119   9 Jan 1741/7 Apr 1742:   Mary ROBINSON -
daughter Elizabeth MCCLENAHAN, nephews Tully and
William ROBINSON, sons of my brother William. Ex:
Tully ROBINSON. Wit: William NIMMO, Christopher
CHAMNEY, William EDGAR.

6DB119   6 Oct 1741/7 Apr 1742:   James WHITE-
HURST - sons James and John, daughters Mary and Mar-
gret. Ex: wife and brother Solomon. Wit: Anthony
WHITEHURST, Thomas WHITEHURST.

6DB120   20 Jan 1741/2/2 Apr 1742:   John PEED -
wife Mary, sons William, John and James. Ex: wife.
Wit: Henry GRIFFIN, Charles GRIFFIN.

6DB133   27 Jan 1741/2/2 Jun 1742:   Francis LAND -
sons John, Francis, Richard, Cornelius and Edward;
daughter Mary, wife Ann. Ex: wife and John WHITE-
HURST. Wit: Edward FRIZZLE, Robert LAND.

6DB135   20 Aug 1741/5 May 1742:   John GALLEY -
wife Blandinah. Ex: wife. Wit: Charles SMYTH,
John EDWARDS.

6DB136 4 Aug 1742: Robert RICHMOND to William and Paul DALE for 6 shillings 100 acres running from the Bay to Long Creek given by Robert RICHMOND, dec. to his son. Wit: James CONDON, Adam DALE, William LOVE.

6DB146 1 Sep 1742: Robert BARTEE and wife Elizabeth (one of daughters and coheirs of Thomas COCKROFT, dec.) to Thomas TAYLOR for 5 shillings fifth part of plantation Thomas COCKROFT lived on. Wit: Arthur SAYER, William NIMMO, Amos MOSELEY.

6DB148 1 Sep 1742: Thomas WISHART to Tully WILLIAMSON for 5 shillings 80 acres near head of Eastern Branch - remainder of 180 acres given by James KEMPE to Thomas and Mary WISHART parents of said Thomas...elder brother James WISHART. Wit: James KEMPE, John COX, William NIMMO.

6DB152 4 Oct 1742: Edward DENBY, millwright and wife Aliff deed of gift to daughter Alice and her husband John HARFORD lot in Newtown. Wit: Thomas WALKE, Arthur SAYER, Robert TODD, William NIMMO, William MOSELEY.

6DB153 21 Feb 1741/2/6 Oct 1742: David SCOTT - brothers John and Walter, sister Mary. Ex: brothers. Wit: James KEMPE, Thomas GRAINGER, William PURDY.

6DB175 22 Sep 1742/1 Oct 1742: Edward IDLE, seaman - wife's brother Henry HOLMES, brother-in-law John HOLMES, Sarah TIMBERLAKE wife of James. Ex: James TIMBERLAKE. Wit: George BALL, George GRIFFEN.

6DB186 25 Jan 1742/3/2 Mar 1742: George SIMMONS - eldest son Thomas, son Lemuel, daughters Mary, Sarah and Easter. Ex: wife. Wit: Patrick MURPHY, Thomas WARD.

6DB193 2 Mar 1742: Daniel and Dinah LENARDto Samuel POWERS of Norfolk for 5 shillings 51 acres upon a branch of Little Creek called Bellomie's Cove - same land granted his father Daniel. Wit: Jonathan MARTIN, Matthew PALLIT.

6DB195 23 Feb 1742/2 Mar 1742: Abraham LEGREW - John KEELING, Honour WOODHOUSE, Ruth SPARKS, Patrick MURPHY and wife. Wit: Patrick MURPHY, John KEELING,Jr.

6DB197 6 Apr 1743? Tully WILLIAMSON to Arthur SAYER for 5 shillings 190 acres that Roger WILLIAMSON give by deed of gift to Tully. Wit: Thomas SPRATT, Emperor MOSELEY.

6DB205 18 Mar 1742/6 Apr 1743: Anne TREVETHAN - grandchildren Elizabeth SCOTT wife of Thomas, Mary Anne THOROWGOOD, Roderick CONNER, Katherine and Stephen WRIGHT, Samuel TENANT; sister Frances CORBETT. Ex: Samuel TENANT. Overseers: William NIMMO, Anthony MOSELEY. Wit: Anne TAINER ___ BURROUGH.

6DB221 4 May 1743: Dorcas BROUGHTON deed of gift to son Edward 25 acres on the Western Shore. Wit: Arthur SAYER, John MUNDEN, Henry BRINSON.

6DB223 16 May 1743/1 Jun 1743: Isaac WHITE -
daughters Sarah and Elizabeth. Ex: brother-in-law
Francis CAREY. Wit: Jacob ELLEGOOD, Sarah CAREY,
Ellen SCOLLEY.

6DB223 2 Apr 1743/1 Jun 1743: Matthew ELLE-
GOOD - son Peter Norley ELLEGOOD, wife Margret,
daughter Mary Anne, sister Sarah, cozen Rebecca
daughter of Sarah ELLEGOOD. Ex: wife and brother
Jacob. Wit: Robert PATTERSON, John MURRELL, Jacob
ELLEGOOD.

6DB227 4 Apr 1743/1 Jun 1743: Lancaster LOVETT -
sons John, William, Lancaster, Henry and Reuben; wife
Mary, daughters Mary and ____. Ex: wife and son John.
Wit: Thomas HENLEY, ____ PALLET, William COX.

6DB233 6 Jul 1743: Richard LESTER, Sr. deed
of gift to brother William OAKHAM, Sr. of 60 acres.
Wit: John RUSSELL, John WHITEHEAD, William CORNICK,
Josiah MORRIS.

6DB234 5 May 1743: Deposition of Augustus
LAND and John SIMMONS of Blackwater that Edward
GIZBURN gave various things to wife Elizabeth and
son Thorowgood.

6DB237 5 Oct 1743: Thomas PURDY, mariner,
son of George to James KEMPE for 15 lbs. half of
plantation George left to sons Thomas and John.
Wit: John THOROWGOOD, William NIMMO, Anthony WALKE,
Jr.

6DB249 7 Dec 1743: Reodolphus MALBONE, mariner of Norfolk Co to Thomas HILL, Sr. and Thomas
HILL, Jr. for 6 shillings 81 acres that he heired
from his father Reodolphus. Wit: John BURFOOT,
Thomas WALKE, William COX.

6DB251 15 Nov 1743/7 Dec 1743: Henry WOOD-
HOUSE - wife Mary, children William, Horatio, Henry
and Mary; daughter Amy HILL, granddaughter Mary HILL.
Ex: wife and son-in-law Charles HILL. Wit: William
COX, ____.

6DB260 21 Feb 1742/1 Feb 1743: Francis ACKISS -
son John (Possum Quarter), son George (plantation
called Holland), wife Anne. Ex: wife and Capt.
James KEMPE. Wit: William NIMMO, James KEMPE.

6DB261 ---/1 Feb 1743: James GRIFFIN - noncupative will - brother Henry, brother John's son
James. Wit: Martha BENTON.

6DB264 30 Jan 1743/4/7 Mar 1743: Andrew PEA-
COCK - wife Ann. Ex: wife. Wit: Solomon MALBONE,
William BONNEY, Jr.

6DB276 7 Mar 1743: William PURDY and wife
Ursilla (one of three sisters and coheirs of Thomas
IVY, dec.) to Arthur SAYER for 5 shillings one third
of plantation where John IVY father of Ursilla lived.
Wit: Anthony MOSELEY, James HUNTER, George WISHART,
James KEMPE.

6DB288 18 Apr 1744/4 Jul 1744: Henry GRIFFEN —
son Henry, wife Margarett. Ex: wife. Wit: Abigail
GRIFFEN, Mahala HOLMES.

6DB288 7 May 1744: Division of estate of William LILBURN, dec. — children Olive and Alexander —
by Nathaniel NEWTON, Anthony MOSELEY, George WISHART.

6DB291 21 Feb 1743/4 Jul 1744: George WEBLIN —
son John (plantation called Codds), wife Mary, daughters Elizabeth, Mary, Hester and Susannah. Ex: wife
and George WEBLIN. Wit: John HARVEY, George WISHART.

6DB292 8 Apr 1743/4 Jul 1744: James FENTRESS —
60 years old when will written — wife Elizabeth, sons
Absalom, James, Horatio and Pharo, daughters Leah,
Elizabeth, Tamer and Sarah Ann. Ex: Thomas WALKE and
Edward MOSELEY. Wit: Michael FENTRESS, Samuel WILES
Absalom FENTRESS.

6DB301 ---/4 Apr 1744: Benjamin COMMINGS OF
Blackwater — sons Martin and Benjamin, wife Elizabeth.
Ex: wife. Wit: John GUISBORN, Richard SMITH.

6DB301 11 Oct --/4 Apr 1744: William CAPPS —
wife Eliza; sons John, Francis, Henry, George, Richard, Horatio and ____; daughter Sarah. Ex: George.
Wit: Solomon WATERMAN, George CAPPS.

6DB309 3 May 1744: Richard CAPPS to George
CAPPS for 6 shillings 40 acres in Muddy Creek heired
from father William. Wit: James NIMMO, James MORE,
John RANEY.

6DB316 3 Sep 1744: William WORMINGTON of Nor-
folk Co deed of gift to sister Grace 120 acres in
Blackwater that father John wanted her to have. Wit:
Sarah BRIGS, Abagall BROOKS, John LOCKHART.

6DB328 2 Mar 1744/4 Jul 1744: John NICHOLAS —
wife, daughters Elizabeth and Ann, sisters Ann and
Elizabeth, brother Isaiah. Ex: Isaiah and cousin
Nathaniel MCCLENAHAN.

6DB358 29 Dec 1744/6 Feb 1744/5: Thomas TAYLOR —
wife Sarah, sons James, William, Thomas and John (plantation in Norfolk Co at head of Julons Creek), daughters Ann, Martha, Mary and Elizabeth. Ex: wife and
Anthony MOSELEY. Wit: Thomas BUTT, Martha BUTT, Jonas
TAYLOR.

6DB361 ---/6 Feb 1744: Thomas WILES — son
Anthony, mariner of Bristol, England; sons Thomas,
Lemuel and Samuel; daughters Sarah, Ann, Mary and
Elizabeth. Ex: Thomas and Lemuel. Wit: Margret
WALKE, John THOROWGOOD, Jr., Anthony WALKE, Jr.,
Edward ATWOOD.

6DB362 8 Feb 1743/6 Feb 1744: Martin BURROUGHS —
Rachel DALE, Elizabeth daughter of William KEELING,
Betty daughter of William DALE, Anthony BURROUGH, Jr.,
Elizabeth daughter of Smith SHIPPERD, William CROMPTON,
cousen Janet BROWN, Ann daughter of Paul DALE, cousen
Ezekiel BROWN, cousen John BROWN, Jr. Ex: John BROWN.
Wit: Robert BURROUGH, William BENSON, Israel KESER,
Adam DALE.

6DB377 6 Mar 1744: Audit of the estate of
Robert RICHMOND by William RICHMOND, Ex.

6DB378 6 Mar 1744: Audit of the estate of William RICHMOND to Capt. William KEELING, Ex.

6DB388 3 Apr 1745: John CAPPS to Thorowgood
BRINSON for 20 lbs. plantation at Muddy Creek - same
land father Richard CAPPS lived on.

6DB390 27 Aug 1742/3 Apr 1745: Capt. Henry MOORE,
Sr. - wife Mary, sons Henry, Thomas, James (Bear Quarter),
Woodhouse, Cason, Anthony (Little Poplar Ridge),John,
Edward and Charles, sister Susana CHESHIRE, daughters
Sarah and Susana. Ex: wife. Wit: Francis MALBONE, Col
Jacob ELLEGOOD.

6DB395 1 May 1745: William RICHMOND to John
RAINEY for 5 sh 50 acres of marsh and sand banks ly-
ing between Lynhaven Bay and Long Creek heired from
his father Robert RICHMOND. Wit: Lemuel CORNICK, John
KEELING, William BODNAM.

6DB397 1 May 1745: William MARTIN and wife Ann
deed of gift to son John ACKISS - if he dies without
issue then to his brother George ACKISS. Wit: Nathaniel
MCCLENAHAN, William ROBINSON.

6DB398 ---/1 May 1745: William SMITH - wife Ann,
daughters Winne, Sarah and Eliza, sons Thomas and Solomon, daughter Susanna SIMPSON. Ex: wife and Solomon.
Wit: John ROBINSON, _____ROBINSON, William BODNAM.

6DB399 1 May 1745: Audit of the estate of Edward GISBURN by Arthur SAYER.

6DB400 1 May 1745: Audit of the estate of William GORNTO to Margret GORNTO, admnx by James CONDON,
Lemuel CORNICK.

6DB406 5 Jun 1745: Mary WALKE now wife of George
WALKE to son James OAST deed of gift of 50 acres heired
from father James SMITH called the Great Pasture. Wit:
James NIMMO, Thomas WISHART, Lewis CONNER.

6DB416 9 Jul 1745/7 Aug 1745: Richard TAYLOR -
son Robert - if without heirs to my sister Mary GRAVE-
NOR. Ex: Arthur SAYER. Wit: ____ WATKINS, Henry
HOLMES, John DAVENPORT.

6DB421 6 Jul 1745: James BROUGHTON and wife Ann
of Norfolk to Dr. George RAMSEY of Norfolk for 6 shillings plantation in Broad Creek devised to Ann by will
of William MARTIN. Wit: James NIMMO, Philip DISON.

6DB425 3 Sep 1745: John AIRS to Solomon WHITE-
HURST for 5 shillings 50 acres - part of same land
Peter CRASHLEY gave to his daughter Ann wife of Michael
eaton. Wit: Arthur SAYER.

6DB429 5 Sep 1745: Appraisal of the estate of
Benoni SMYTH by Thomas WALKE, Edward HACK MOSELEY,
William PARSONS.

6DB431 25 Dec 1740/4 Sep 1745: Ann COLLINS -
daughter Sarah, son George. Ex: brother Mark POWELL.
wit: Presson MARTIN, Samuel BOUSH.

6DB449 6 Nov 1745: George EILAND and wife
Sarah to Samuel MACASSLON, feltmaker, for 5 shillings 300 acres called Black Charles heired from
Richard EILAND. Wit: John HEATH, Richard MORSE,
Richard MCCLURE, John BURFOOT, Charles SMYTH, William KEELING, Sr., Philip DYSON, John KEELING.
    6DB460 ---/6 Nov 1745: Henry WOODHOUSE, mari-
ner - noncupative will - prize money to Mrs. Mary
WOODHOUSE. Wit: John FLEAR, Sarah SIMMONS.
    6DB464 19 Dec 1742/6 Nov 1745: Richard LESTER
- daughter Isabel, sons Richard, John, Abel and Wil-
liam, wife Dorcas. Ex: wife. Wit: William OAKHAM,
John RUSSEL.
    6DB465 22 Aug 1745/6 Nov 1745: Paul RIGBY -
child wife goes with, Martha MORSE wife of Thomas,
Joyce SCARBORRE wife of Charles, Ann SENICA daughter of Nathaniel, William PARSONS, Nathaniel SENICA.
Ex: John WHITEHEAD. Wit: John MURPHY, Dinah WARD,
Omey PATTERSON.
    6DB466 6 Nov 1745: John HARPER the Elder to
son John half of plantation known as Ashen Swamp.
Wit: Thomas WALKE, Edward DENBY, James NIMMO.
    6DB467 3 Dec 1745: Cason BUSKY and wife Mary
(only daughter of John and Elizabeth CANNON who was
one of two sisters and coheirs of Edward LAND, Jr.,
dec.) to Col. Anthony WALKE for 5 shillings half of
100 acres - same land Edward LAND the Elder left to
his son Edward LAND, Jr. Wit: Arthur SAYER, William
PURDY, James SMYTH
    6DB471 3 Dec 1745: William PURDY and wife Ur-
silla (one of daughters of John IVY, dec. and one of
two sisters and coheirs of Aliph late wife of Matthias MILLER, mariner of Norfolk Co) to Arthur SAYER
for 5 shillings half part of one undivided third part
of 600 acres which John IVY left to his son Thomas
who died without heirs and so it was divided between
his sisters Ursilla, Aliph and Hannah. Wit: James
KEMPE, Archibald MCCULL.
    6DB475 3 Dec 1745: William COX and wife Ann
(one of daughters and coheirs of William LOVETT, dec.)
to Thomas WALKE for 2 shillings 50 acres hear the
head of Bowrin's River. Wit: Thomas HUNTER, Nathaniel MCCLENAHAN.
    6DB482 4 Dec 1745: Appraisal of the estate of
John JAMESON.
    6DB483 4 Dec 1745: Inventory of the estate of
Richard LESTER by Dorcas LESTER.
    6DB483 4 Dec 1745: Inventory of Paul RIGBY by
John BONNEY, Erasmus HAYNES, John MORSE.
    6DB484 4 Dec 1745: Audit of the estate of
Baron MORSE by Arthur SAYER, James KEMPE.
    6DB491 20 Nov 1745/1 Jan 1745: Solomon WATER-
MAN - sons Charles and Solomon, daughters Mary and
Francis, wife. Ex: wife. Wit: Peter MORRISETT,
James MOORE, _____ MOORE.

6DB500 5 Feb 1745: Audit of the estate of Henry and Ann COLLINS by James KEMPE, George WISHART.

6DB501 8 Aug 1745/5 Feb 1745: William BONNEY - sons John and Thomas, daughters Jean and Betty, wife. Ex: wife. Wit: Charles HENLEY, Grace HENLEY.

6DB501 1 Feb 1741/5 Feb 1745: Nathaniel LILBURN, mariner now taking a voyage to sea - sisters Katherine and Olive, brother Alexander, Henry CHAPMAN son of Nickles CHAPMAN. Ex: Josiah SMYTH. Wit: Matthias MILLER, Cason MOORE.

6DB502 5 Feb 1745: Inventory of the estate of Mrs. Mary MOORE by William KEELING, Jr., William COX, Lemuel CORNICK.

6DB507 5 Mar 1745: Willis PARSONS and wife Dinah to Tully MOSELEY 50 acres at head of Gum Swamp given Dinah by her grandfather. Wit: Emperor MOSELEY, Samuel BOUSH, John THOROWGOOD, Jr.

6DB510 5 Mar 1745: Appraisal of the estate of Philip DYSON by John THOROWGOOD, Jr., Thomas HUNTER, George WEBLIN.

6DB511 2 Apr 1746: Inventory of the estate of Nathaniel LILBURN by Tully ROBINSON SMITH, Edward HACK MOSELEY, William HANCOCK and Tully ROBINSON.

6DB519 24 Mar 1745/6: Appraisal of the estate of Martin BURROUGH to John BROWN, Ex. by Joel CORNICK, John JAMES, Edward ATTWOOD.

6DB522 20 May 1746: Mary BRAY (one of the daughters and coheirs of Edward BRAY) to Tully ROBINSON SMYTH for 33 lbs. 6 shillings one third part of 200 acres on Broad Creek. Wit: Thomas WALKE, William HANCOCK.

6DB534 5 Mar 1745: William SUTTON WHITE to William COX for 6 shillings 105 acres - same land held by his father Joseph. Wit: Kiteley ROE, Henry MOORE, Charles MALBONE, Charles SMYTH, William ROBINSON.

6DB534 21 Apr 1747: Elizabeth WHITE, widow of Joseph WHITE relinquishes her right of dower.

6DB537 19 Feb 1745/20 May 1746: John SMITH of Blackwater - sons Samuel, John and Seth, wife Elizabeth. Ex: wife. Wit: Peter HARBERT, William DELYMILL, Bernard BANGER, John GUISBORN.

6DB538 3 Feb 1745/2 May 1746: Benony HEATH - brother Jacobus, son James, wife Vilate. Ex: wife. Wit: Peter HARBERT, John GISBORN, Bernard BANGER.

6DB539 15 Mar 1737/8/20 May 1746: Martha CREED - daughters Mary BRAY, Martha ROBINSON, Dinah CAPPS and Easter FISHER, children John and Rebecah CREED. Ex: son-in-law John BRAY and John BONNEY. Wit: Lancaster LOVETT, John BERRY, John BONNEY, Sr.

6DB556 17 Jun 1746: Audit of the estate of William DAVIS by Arthur SAYER and James KEMPE.

6DB556 17 Jun 1746: Audit of the estate of
John HUGINS by Nathaniel NEWTON, James KEMPE and
George WISHART.

6DB557 17 Apr 1746/17 Jun 1746: Robert DUDLEY -
sons Robert and Henry, daughters Jasabellah, Amy and
Eliza, brother Thomas, Eliza JACKSON, wife Eliza.
Ex. wife. Wit: Willis SIMMONS, Cornelius AUSTIN,
Henry WHITE.

6DB557 17 Jun 1746: Lemuel WHITEHURST to Richard DAVIS, ship carpenter of Norfolk for 37 lbs. 16
shillings 150 acres devised to him by the will of his
father Thomas. Wit: Abel LEWELLING, John WILLIAMSON,
David MURRAY.

6DB562 15 Jul 1746: Richard GARNOR and wife
Eliza deed of gift to daughter Mary 80 acres called
Creedles. Wit: William CONSAUL, Sr., William CON-
SAUL, Jr., Zacharias BOUSH.

6DB578 3 Dec 1745/15 Jul 1746: William BODNAM -
wife Kezia. Ex: wife. Wit: Joel CORNICK, William
SMITH.

6DB578 15 Jul 1746: Sarah TAYLOR deed of gift
to children Randall JONES and Ann TAYLOR. Wit: Arthur
SAYER, Anthony LAWSON.

6DB585 6 May 1746/19 Aug 1746: William GISBURN -
brother Edward, daughter Mary, wife Mary. Ex: wife
and father Giles RANDOLPH. Wit: John GISBORN, James
RANDOLPH, Willis WHITEHEAD.

6DB586 24 Apr 1746/19 Aug 1746: Richard SMYTH
of Blackwater - sons Richard and James, daughter Sarah,
wife Eliza. Ex: wife and son Richard. Wit: John GIS-
BORN, Edmond DOE, Eliza OLIVER.

6DB591 16 Sep 1746: George PURDY of Norfolk Co,
mariner to James HUNTER for 40 lbs. 47 acres on the
Western Shore whichGeorge PURDY, Sr. left to his son.
Wit: James KEMPE, William PURDY, Arthur SAYER, Dinah
CHAPMAN.

6DB596 16 Sep 1746: Inventory and appraisal of
the estate of James WILLIAMSON by Nathaniel MCCLENA-
HAN, Tully ROBINSON, Edward DENBY.

6DB598 21 Oct 1746: Capt. John THOROWGOOD to
William NASH, ship carpenter of Norfolk for 5 shil-
lings 448 acres left by his father John known as
Puggett's Neck. Wit: Nathaniel NEWTON, Anthony LAWSON.

6DB601 21 Oct 1746: Anthony WHITEHURST to Moses
FENTRESS son of John FENTRESS, dec. for 5 shillings
50 acres at Three Runns. Wit: William PORTLOCK, Job
GASKINGS, Jr.

6DB604 21 Oct 1746: Audit of the estate of
William MOSELEY by William HANCOCK, Nathaniel MCCLE_
NAHAN, Tully ROBINSON.

6DB613 16 Sep 1746: Inventory and appraisal of
Mrs. Margret ELLEGOOD by Robert PATTERSON, William
KEELING, Jr., Lemuel CORNICK.

6DB614 ----/16 Dec 1746: Sarah HARVAY - non-cupative will - Thomas HUNTER. Wit: Eliza OMERRY, Sarah TOMLINGSON.

6DB621 20 Jan 1746: William KEELING, Jr. and wife Mary (one of two daughters and coheirs of John THOROWGOOD) for 5 shillings half of 750 acres in the Western Shore. Wit: William KEELING, Sr., William COX, Nathaniel MCCLENAHAN.

6DB629 20 Jan 1746: William ROBINSON to William KEELING, Jr. for 200 lbs. 200 acres in the Eastern Shore given him by his father William. Wit: William KEELING, Sr., William COX, Nathaniel MCCLE-NAHAN.

6DB632 11 Nov 1746/20 Jan 1746: Thomas SPRATT - wife Mary. Ex: wife. Wit: John RUSSELL, Amy WEST, Henry SPRATT.

6DB632 13 Jun 1746/20 Jan 1746: John MARSHALL - wife Pembrook - at her decease to be divided between her two eldest sons. Ex: wife and Capt. William KEELING. Wit: Henry DAULEY, John CAPPS, Thomas LANGLEY.

6DB633 16 Dec 1746: Audit of the estate of John WISHART.

6DB634 24 Mar 1745/6/17 Feb 1746: Lemuel THELABALL now going to sea - brothers Lewis, Nathaniel and Thomas. Ex: Lewis and Thomas. Wit: James SMITH, Henry SNAILE.

6DB635 17 Feb 1746: Sarah CONDON deed of gift to son-in-law Robert PATERSON. Wit: Lemuel CORNICK, Lancaster LOVETT, Jacob ELLEGOOD.

6DB636 17 Feb 1746: Appraisal of the estate of Capt. James CONDON by Jacob ELLEGOOD, Lemuel CORNICK, William KEELING, Jr.

6DB652 17 Mar 1746: John BUSKEY to son William and grandson John son of Cason BUSKEY alias KEELING deed of gift. Wit: Jacob ELLEGOOD, Rebecah ELLEGOOD.

6DB653 17 Mar 1746: Audit of Francis MOSELEY by Nathaniel NEWTON, James KEMPE, Tully ROBINSON.

6DB654 17 Mar 1746: Audit of the estate of Elizabeth GUISBURN by Jacob ELLEGOOD, Lemuel CORNIK, Robert PATERSON.

6DB662 23 Feb 1746/16 Jun 1747: Nathaniel NICHOLAS - wife Sarah, daughter Mary, son Nathaniel. Ex: wife. Wit: Arthur SAYER, James KEMPE.

6DB669 23 May 1747/16 Jun 1747: William WEBLIN - wife Sarah, brother George. Wit: Richard DUDLEY, Sr., Richard DUDLEY, Jr.

6DB670 16 Jun 1747: Audit of the estate of George BOUSH by Arthur SAYER.

6DB672 16 Jun 1747: Yates NICHOLAS admnx to John NICHOLAS deed of gift to daughters Elizabeth and Anne. Wit: Thomas WALKE, Jonathan SAUNDERS, Edward DENBY.

6DB683   18 Aug 1747:   Audit of the estate of Thomas CLAY by Arthur SAYER, James KEMPE, Thomas WALKE.

6DB683   17 Nov 1747:   Inventory of the estate of Charles HENLEY by John BONNEY, Sr., Tully WILLIAMSON, Peter B. MALBONE.

6DB684   18 Aug 1747:   Audit of the estate of James WILLIAMSON by Nathaniel MCCLENAHAN, James KEMPE, Tully ROBINSON.

6DB685   15 Sep 1747:   Thomas MOORE and wife Sarah to Robert JONES for 80 lbs 125 acres which Capt. Henry MOORE devised to his son Thomas.   Wit: John BURFOOT, John BRINSON, Lemuel BOUSH.

6DB687   14 Sep 1747:   William GASTON and wife Mary to John TURNER for 15 lbs. half of plantation William CARTWRIGHT father of Mary lived on.   Wit: Arthur SAYER.

6DB689   15 Sep 1747:   Audit of the estate of John BARNES by Arthur SAYER.

6DB697   20 Oct 1747:   Audit of the estate of Richard TAYLOR by James KEMPE, Nathaniel MCCLENAHAN, Tully ROBINSON.

6DB708   29 Sep 1747/17 Nov 1747:   Charles HENLEY - wife, son John, daughters Frances, Sarah and Mary. Ex: son John and great John HENLEY.   Wit: James CASON, John BROWN, Sarah CASON.

6DB713   25 Jan 1745/17 Nov 1747:   Henry SOUTHERN - son Henry, daughter Elizabeth.   Ex: children.   Wit: William MAUSON, Obediah MOORE, Benony HEATH.

6DB714   17 Nov 1747:   Anthony WALKE deed of gift to son Anthony 274 acres.   Wit: Samuel HOLLOWELL, William MALBONE.

6DB716   ---/19 Jan 1747:   Woodhouse MOORE, taking a voyage - father Henry, brother Cason.   Wit: Alexander CRAKIN, Thomas WILSON.

6DB718   30 Sep 1747/19 Jan 1747:   John NICHOLAS - Samuel BOUSH, brother Nathaniel.   Ex: Samuel BOUSH. Wit: John THOROWGOOD, Jr., Jonathan SAUNDERS, Lemuel EWELL.

DEED BOOK SEVEN

7DB3   1 Jun 1747/15 Mar 1747:   Jonathan MARTIN -
wife, sons Preson and James, daughter Kezzia. Wit:
Henry JAMESON, Jonathan MARTIN, Thomas OWENS.
7DB3   17 Apr 1748:   Inventory of the estate of
Capt. William COX by William KEELING, Sr., Lemuel
CORNICK.
7DB8   23 Mar 1747/8:   John BRINSON to James
CARROWAY for 52 lbs. 10 shillings 70 acres on the
Eastern Shore which his father Thomas bought of
John RANEY. Wit: William CARTWRIGHT, William MOYE,
Charles MALBONE
7DB9   6 Oct 1747/19 Apr 1748:   William SPANN -
wife Anne, daughters Dinah and Mary. Ex: wife and
son-in-law John LINAHAN. Wit: Ann JONES, Erasmus
HAYNES.
7DB16   28 Dec 1747/17 May 1748:   Edward KEELING
- brother William. Wit: John GILES, William COX,
William CROMPTON.
7DB17   17 May 1748:   Appraisal of the estate of
Elizabeth GISBURN by Kiteley ROE, Adam TOOLY, Lawrence DOYLEY.
7DB17   17 May 1748:   Appraisal of the estate of
Sarah SMYTH by James KEMPE, James HUNTER, Edward
DENBY.
7DB17   17 May 1748:   Inventory of the estate
of William SPANN·
7DB20   21 Jun 1748:   Appraisal of the estate
of William LOVETT by Joel CORNICK, Adam HAYES, John
MUNDEN.
7DB21   21 Jun 1748:   Thomas MOORE to Matthew
PALLET for 6 shillings 30 acres which Henry MOORE
devised to his son Thomas. Wit: Edward DENBY, William DALE, Samuel BOUSH.
7DB22   21 Jun 1748:   Appraisal of the estate
of Edward KEELING by Lemuel CORNICK, Charles HILL,
John MOORE.
7DB24   19 Jul 1748:   James CARROWAY to James
LOVETT for 5 shillings 100 acres in the North Woods
- part of a patent granted to John CARROWAY. Wit:
John BRINSON, Adam LOVETT.
7DB27   7 Jul 1748:   Appraisal of the estate of
Peter MORRISET by John BONNEY, Sr., Tully WILLIAM-
SON, Peter MALBONE, William DYER.

7DB37   16 Aug 1748:   Inventory of the estate of Thomas LAMOUNT by Lemuel CORNICK, Joel CORNICK.

7DB37   16 Aug 1748:   Appraisal of the estate of Jeremiah HENLY by Joel CORNICK, John MUNDEN, John GORNTO, Jr.

7DB37   20 Sep 1748:   Appraisal of the estate of John HARRISON by Joel CORNICK, William KEELING.

7DB42   20 Sep 1748:   Dennis CANNON to John CAPPS for 5 shillings 200 acres which Edward CANNON, Sr. gave to his sons Edward and Dennis. Wit: Henry DAULEY, William DAULEY, Dennis DAULEY.

7DB45   16 Aug 1748:   John MERCER and wife Martha, Elias WELLS and wife Jane and Frances CONDON (sisters and coheirs of Capt. James CONDON) to Jacob ELLEGOOD for 6 shillings 180 acres in the Eastern Shore and 250 acres of swamp. Wit: James KEMPE, Lemuel CORNICK, George WISHART, Thomas WALKE, William KEELING, Francis LAND.

7DB48   18 Oct 1748:   William CONSAUL to son William deed of gift of 150 acres. Wit: William PURDY, John MOORE, John BRINSON.

7DB48   5 Sep 1741:   Elizabeth MCCLENAHAN - grandchildren Nathaniel, David and Anne MCCLENAHAN and Elizabeth MCCLENAHAN ROBINSON, Tully and William ROBINSON sons of William, Elizabeth daughter of John NICHOLAS. Ex: John NICHOLAS, Jr. and Natheniel MCCLENAHAN. Wit: James WILLIAMSON, Ann HANCOCK, Ann WILLIAMSON.

7DB51   15 Nov 1748:   Thomas MOORE deed of gift to children Edmond and Elizabeth after death of wife Sarah. Wit: Robert PATERSON, James MOORE.

7DB53   3 Oct 1748/15 Nov 1748:   Adam HAYES - brothers Lemuel GASKING (Blackwarned Ridge), Henry GASKING and Charles GASKING, Edward HOLMES, sister Sarah GASKING. Ex: brother Charles. Wit: Henry LAMOUNT, Adam LOVETT, Job GASKING, Jr.

7DB56   20 Dec 1748:   John WILLIAMSON, Sr. deed of gift to son-in-law George CAPPS of 50 acres. Wit: Thomas WALKE, Charles GASKING.

7DB56   20 Dec 1748:   Audit of the estate of Thomas WALSTON by Arthur SAYER, Tully ROBINSON.

7DB58   20 Dec 1748:   William PURDY son of George, dec. to George JAMESON, blacksmith for 5 lbs. 200 acres on the South side of the Eastern Branch. Wit: Edward HACK MOSELEY, Robert BOYDE, John INCE, Jr.

7DB59   14 Nov 1748/20 Dec 1748:   Thomas HUDDLESTONE Elder - daughters Amy CANNON, Dina, Barbara CAVENDER, Elizabeth RANEY and Mary JONES; sons John and Thomas. Ex: son Thomas. Wit: Joel CORNICK, James BANNISTER, Edward PETTY.

7DB63   20 Dec 1748:   Capt. Solomon EDEY and wife Hannah to Arthur SAYER for 5 shillings half of 600 acres where Hannah's father John IVY lived. Wit: James MOORE, Lemuel CORNICK, William KEELING, Jr.

7DB67   13 Sep 1743/20 Dec 1748:   Richard DUDLEY
- son Daniel, daughter Frances, wife Mary all my
children. Ex: wife. Wit: Anthony MOSELEY, Mary
LESTER, Frances MUNTGOMERY.

7DB72   20 Dec 1748:   Inventory of the estate
of Elizabeth MCCLENAHAN by Nathaniel MCCLENAHAN.

7DB74   17 Jan 1748:   Thomas LANGLEY deed of
gift to wife Bridget. Wit: James WHITEHURST, John
SNAILE.

7DB74   22 Jul 1748/17 Jan 1748:   Willis WHITE-
HURST - brothers Arthur and Charles. Ex: brothers.
Wit: John SMYTH, Mary BOUSH.

7DB82   21 Jul 1748:   Inventory of the estate
of Thomas SPRATT by Dennis DAULEY.

7DB88   21 Mar 1748:   Edward SHARPE and wife
Dinah (one of three sisters and coheirs of John
GOODACRE) to George WEBLIN 90 acres near Thurston's
Bridge on the Western Shore. Wit: Job GASKING, John
HENLEY, Charles MALBONE.

7DB89   21 Mar 1748:   Israel SLATTER and wife
Lidia to Kiteley ROE for 60 lbs. 100 acres in Black-
water formerly belonging to George BUCK father of
Lidia. Wit: Luke SLATTER, Thomas OLDS, Matthias
MILLER, Elinor ROE.

7DB96   20 Dec 1748/21 Mar 1748:   John MOORE -
mother Anne COX; brothers William, Benjamin and
Jonathan COX, four sisters Mary Boush, Anne, Elizabeth and Amy CO X. Ex: mother. Wit: William KEE-
LING, Jr., William CROMPTON.

7DB96   21 Mar 1748:   Inventory of the estate
of Richard DUDLEY.

7DB96   21 Mar 1748:   Richard BELL to his ser-
vant Elizabeth HILL, an Indian woman, and her son
David, discharge from service. Wit: Edward BONNEY,
Cason MOORE, Jr.

7DB101   1 Apr 1749:   Audit of the estate of
Mrs. Sarah SMYTH by William HANCOCK, Tully ROBINSON.

7DB104   30 Sep 1748/6 May 1749:   Mary WHITE-
HURST - sons Thomas, Anthony and Solomon, grandson
John son of James WHITEHURST, grandson William son
of Anthony WHITEHURST, daughter Elizabeth EATON,
grandsons Michael and James EATON, grandson Godfrey
son of Thomas WHITEHURST, grandson James son of James
WHITEHURST, grandson John son of William WHITEHURST,
daughters Dinah CAPPS and Sarah HENLEY. Ex: son
Thomas. Wit: John CUMBERFOOT, Mary CUMBERFOOT, Cason
MOORE, Jr.

7DB105   16 May 1749:   Margrette MALBONE deed
of gift to grandchildren Godfrey, John, Alif and
Margrette MALBONE. Wit: Edward BONNEY, John DEER-
MORE, Cason MOORE, Jr.

7DB105   13 Mar 1748/16 May 1749: Henry SPRATT -
brother James, John GREEN, cousins Frances, Mary and
Catey WHITE. Ex: brother Patrick WHITE. Wit: William OKEHAM, Thomas GIBBS.

7DB106 21 Jan 1748/9: Thomas GRANTE - wife Mary, daughter Onner, James EATON, Mary EASTER. Wit: Henry JAMESON, Thomas OWENS, Alexander JAMESON.

7DB109 12 Apr 1749/20 Jun 1749: Bartholomew WILLIAMSON - wife Dinah; sons James, Robert, Joshua and John; daughters Prudence, Mary and Dinah. Ex: wife. Wit: Henry SNAIL, Sarah SNAILE, Mary DAY.

7DB111 18 Jul 1749: Inventory of the estate of Henry SPRATT by John BONNEY, Sr., Tully WILLIAM-SON, John RUSSELL.

7DB112 18 Jul 1749: Thorowgood SPRATT deed of gift to sons Henry and Argall after decease of wife Mary, daughter Mary. Wit: Thomas CANNON, Anthony BARNS.

7DB113 18 Jul 1749: Audit of the estate of Thomas LAMOUNT by Joel CORNICK, William KEELING.

7DB113 18 Jul 1749: Inventory of the estate of Thomas HUDDLESTON by Thomas HUDDLESTON, Jr.

7DB126 19 Jan 1749: Thomas CORNICK of Knotts Island deed of gift to son Elias 200 acres. Wit: Robert DUDLEY, Henry DUDLEY, William MACKIE.

7DB131 19 Sep 1749: Joel SIMMONS, boatwright to John son of Francis and Amy THOROWGOOD, mariner for 5 shillings 46 acres on the Eastern Shore. Wit: Thomas HAYNES, Samuel BOUSH.

7DB132 15 Sep 1748/19 Sep 1749: John AIRS - sons Willoby and John, John RANEY, wife Ruth, daughters Elizabeth, Ruth, Mary and Martha. Ex: wife and John BONNEY, Wit: John RANEY, Thomas WHITEHURST, Cason MOORE, Jr.

7DB140 24 Sep 1747/21 Nov 1749: William DYER - sons William and Hezekiah, daughters Elizabeth and Mary, wife Elizabeth. Ex: wife. Wit: John WILLIAMSON, Thomas WILLIAMSON, Cason MOORE, Jr.

7DB141 14 Oct 1749: Inventory of the estate of John AIRES by John BONNEY, Jr. Cason MOORE, Jr.

7DB141 ---/21 Nov 1749: Dinah SULLIVAN - noncupative will - son Manuel BUTT, sons John and Moses SULLIVAN. Wit: Thomas TURNER, Mark ROBERTS.

7DB142 16 Jan 1749: Inventory of the estate of Bartholomew WILLIAMSON by John CHAPMAN.

7DB145 30 May 1746/16 Jan 1749: Susanah CHE-SHIRE - son John THOROWGOOD, daughter Pembrook wife of Capt. Stephen WRIGHT, daughter Elizabeth. Ex: Capt. Stephen WRIGHT, Capt. Arthur SAYER and daughter Elizabeth. Wit: Thomas WALKE, Monica CONNER, Anthony WALKE, Anthony WALKE, Jr.

7DB146 16 Jan 1749: Willis WHITEHEAD to John WHITEHURST for 2 shillings 60 acres at Matchepungo heired from father Charles. Wit: John WHITEHEAD, James MASON, Thomas TORTON.

7DB150 16 Jul 1749: Inventory of the estate of William DYER by Elizabeth DYER.

7DB153 20 Mar 1749: Richard DROUGHT - mother Mary LESTER, sister-in-law Amy LESTER, Rebecka daughter of Robert and Amy MOSELEY, Mary daughter of George and Mary WISHART. Ex: mother. Wit: George WISHART, Robert MOSELEY.

7DB155 20 Mar 1749: Caleb WHITEHURST deed of gift to Enoch WHITEHURST 50 acres which his father Hugh WHITEHURST gave to him. Wit: Arthur SAYER, James KEMPE, George WISHART, Edmond ABSALOM.

7DB157 20 Mar 1749: Charles NICHOLSON son and heir of Thomas NICHOLSON to Anthony WALKE for 200 lbs. 27 acres. Wit: Josiah BUTT, William MALBONE, Anthony MOSELEY, George WISHART, Charles GASKING, John DOYLEY.

7DB161 2 Nov 1749/20 Mar 1749: Charles SMYTH of Newtown, merchant - wife Margrett, sons Tully and Perrin, daughters Betty, Margrett and Anne. Ex: wife and Arthur SAYER. Wit: Thomas GRAINGER, George WEBLIN.

7DB166 ---/20 Mar 1749: Robert WHITEHURST - wife Florance, son Anthony, daughter Mary, rest of my children. Wit: Anthony BURROUGH, Christopher MOSELEY, ____ WHITEHURST.

7DB166 10 Mar 1749/20 Mar 1749: Margret JOHNSON - daughter Mary wife of Capt. James NIMMO, daughter Jacomine wife of John HUNTER, grandson Jacob HUNTER. Ex: sons-in-law Capt. James NIMMO and John HUNTER. Wit: Arthur SAYER, John HARPER, Thomas HARVEY.

7DB167 20 Mar 1749: Inventory of the estate of Susannah CHESHIRE.

7DB167 20 Mar 1749: Appraisal of the estate of John HARPER by John HUNTER, John THOROWGOOD, Sr., Adam THOROWGOOD.

7DB167 - Dec 1749/20 Mar 1749: Marting CUMMINGS - brothers Joshua, Caleb and Benjamin, mother Elizabeth. Ex: mother. Wit: ____ DAVIS, Henry GISBORN.

7DB168 6 Jan 1749/50/20 Mar 1749: John DYER - sons William and John, wife Sarah, five children John, James, Sarah, Lydia and Jemima. Ex: wife. Wit: Solomon WHITEHURST, Sarah WHITEHURST, Cason MOORE, Jr.

7DB168 6 Apr 1740/15 May 1750: John TURNER - Lemuel CARTWRIGHT, Thomas TURNER, William SALMONS, Lewis PRICE, Job GASKING, John son of Tully WILLIAMSON, Francis (?) son of Tully WILLIAMSON, Mary daughter of Tully WILLIAMSON, her brother Henry, Sarah CARTWRIGHT daughter of Mary BARROT, Anthony WILLIAMSON, child Elizabeth PRICE goes with, Mary BARROT. Ex: ____ GASKING, Jr, Lemuel CARTWRIGHT. Wit: James CARRAWAY, Mary CARTWRIGHT.

7DB169   15 May 1750:   Appraisal of the estate
of James JONES by Thomas WISHART, James ASHLEY,
Presson MARTIN.

7DB169. 15 May 1750:   Audit of the estate of
Doyley LATTER by Arthur SAYER.

7DB169   - Dec 1749/15 May 1750:   William DALE -
wife Elizabeth, daughter Betty, Mary DALE alias MC-
BRIDE daughter of Ruth MCBRIDE, Mary, Anne and Rachel
daughters of Mary MCBRIDE.   Wit: Mary Anne DALE and
Jacob ELLEGOOD.

7DB170   15 May 1750:   John WILLIS and wife Margret, heir to William GORNTO and Margret GORNTO,
widow, to John GORNTO for 5 shillings 50 acres William GORNTO died possessed of.   Wit: John GORNTO,
John WILLIS, Thomas FINKLEY.

7DB172   15 May 1750:   Inventory of the estate
of John DYER by Sarah DYER.

7DB176   ---/15 May 1750:   Patience BURROUGH -
noncupative will - sons Argall and Adam THOROWGOOD,
Betty and Abigal daughters of Adam.   Wit: Anne RICE,
Barbara MUNO, Elizabeth PRICKET.

7DB181   19 Jun 1750:   Richard LESTER to William
CORNICK for 5 shillings 50 acres given him by deed
of gift from his father Richard LESTER, dec.   Wit:
John WHITEHEAD, Jr., James MASON, William WHITEHEAD.

7DB186   19 Jun 1750:   John MUNDAY and wife Mary
to James ASHLEY for 25 lbs. 125 acres which descended to said Mary as being one of the daughters of
Robert HOLMES.   Wit: William NIMMO, Henry JAMESON,
_____, Tully MOSELEY.

7DB190   7 Feb 1749/50:   Mark POWELL to William
ROBINSON for 5 shillings 95 acres on the Western
Shore which Mark's father Mark bought of William
GRANT.   Wit: Arthur SAYER, Thomas HAYNES, _____
SAUNDERS, William JACOB.

7DB192   2 Jul 1750/17 Jul 1750:   John WILLIAMS,.
Sr. - wife Elizabeth, sons John and Solomon, wife's
son John CAPPS.   Son Thomas and daughter Mary CARREL
have received their portions.   Ex: wife and son John.
Wit: Dennis DAWLEY, Mary WILLIAMS, Cason MOORE.

7DB196   21 Aug 1750:   Inventory of the estate
of James BLAIR by Adam TOOLY, John WICKERS, John
GISBURN.

7DB196   29 Dec 1749/21 Aug 1750:   William WIGGIN
- son Francis, son-in-law Edward MOSELEY, wife.   Ex:
wife.   Wit: John MONTGOMERE, Robert MOSELEY.

7DB196   21 Aug 1750:   Appraisal of the estate
of John NICHOLAS by John HUNTER, John THOROWGOOD,
Sr., Adam THOROWGOOD.

7DB197   21 Aug 1750:   Audit of the estate of
Francis ACKISS by Thomas WALKE, Nathaniel MCCLEN-
AHAN, Tully ROBINSON.

7DB205   15 Oct 1750:   Inventory of the estate of John MOORE by Robert PATERSON, Lemuel CORNICK.

7DB205   16 Oct 1750:   Audit of the estate of John HARRISON by Joel CORNICK, John BONNEY, Sr.

7DB207   20 Nov 1750:   James SMITH to Charles HICHOLSON for 100 lbs. 127 acres where John SMITH, father of James lived - part purchased by William SMITH, the Elder and part deed of gift to John SMITH from John WHITEHURST, Sr. Wit: Thomas WALKE, William JACOB.

7DB209   20 Nov 1750:   Inventory of the estate of Robert WHITEHURST.

7DB209   15 Jan 1750:   Appraisal of the estate of John HARPER, Sr. by John HUNTER, John THOROWGOOD, Sr., Adam THOROWGOOD.

7DB212   18 Dec 1750:   John LAMOUNT deed of gift to wife Lidia. Wit: Joseph HILL, Anthony MOSELEY, John BURFOOT.

7DB214   22 Mar 1749/50/18 Dec 1750:   James GISBORN - sons John, James and Solomon, daughter Sarah, wife Elizabeth. Ex: wife. Wit: ___ ETHEREDGE, Thomas GISBORN, Augustus LANE, James GISBORN.

7DB214   11 Nov 1750/18 Dec 1750:   Elenor JONES - Anne BURGESS daughter of Henry, Henry BURGESS. Ex: Henry BURGESS. Wit: Batson WHITEHURST, Sr., Batson WHITEHURST, Jr.

7DB217   15 Nov 1750:   Anthony LAWSON deed of gift to Thomas LAWSON 400 acres given by father Thomas. Wit: ___ NEWTON, James NIMMO, Gershom NIMMO.

7DB221   13 Nov 1750/15 Jan 1750:   William PURDY - sons Evan, Hugh and William, daughters Dinah WARD and Mary. Ex: sons William and Evan. Wit: John SENICA, James SENICA.

7DB225   19 Jul 1750:   Samuel WILBUR deed of gift to brother John land near Borrin's River on the southwest side of the Cypress Swamp. Wit: Arthur SAYER James KEMPE, Thomas WALKE.

7DB227   19 Feb 1740:   Samuel WILBUR deed of brother Francis land on Bowring's River - same land John WILBUR, dec. exchanged with Richard LAND. Wit: Arthur SAYER, James KEMPE, Thomas WALKE.

7DB229   19 Feb 1750:   Thomas LANGLEY, Jr. deed of gift to wife Bridget. Wit: John WHITEHURST, Thomas CASON.

7DB231   7 Oct 1748/19 Feb 1750:   John KEY - sons John and James, daughter Sarah, sons Joseph, Joshua and Jonathan, daughter Anne BATSON. Ex: son James. Wit: Robert BURROUGH, Mary GILCRIST(?).

7DB233   19 Feb 1750:   Appraisal of the estate of Thomas HILL by Joel CORNICK, Lemuel CORNICK, William WOODHOUSE.

7DB236   4 Jan 1750/51/19 Feb 1750:   Roger WIL-
LIAMSON - sons Tully, Samuel, James, Solomon, Anthony
and Rodger, daughter Elizabeth COOPER. Ex: sons
Roger and Solomon. Wit: Thomas GRAINGER, Maximillian
BOUSH, John WILLIAMSON.

7DB239   19 Feb 1750:   Inventory of the estate
of William WIGGENS.

7DB245   16 Jan 1750/1/19 Mar 1750:   Smith SHE-
PARD - wife Frances, daughters Frances and Elizabeth,
sons Smith and William. Wit: Lemuel CORNICK, Adam
DALE.

7DB247   31 Jul 1747/19 Mar 1750:   Thomas FRANK-
LIN - sons Daniel and Thomas, daughter Mary, wife
Sarah. Ex: wife. Wit: Elizabeth SPANN, _____,
John BONNEY, Sr.

7DB248   19 Mar 1750:   Inventory of the estate
of John KEY by Lemuel CORNICK, Lancaster LOVETT.

7DB248   19 Mar 1750:   Inventory of the estate
of Michael SHERWOOD by Elizabeth SHEARWOOD.

7DB250   7 Nov 1750/16 Apr 1751:   Samuel POWER -
wife Mary, sons Samuel and Joseph, daughter Amy,
four daughters Elizabeth, Mary and two not yet bap-
tized. Ex: wife. Wit: Thomas OWENS, Robbard OLD-
NER, James ASHLEY.

7DB252   16 Apr 1751:   Inventory of the estate
of Thomas FRANKLIN by Erasmus HAYNES, John BONNEY,
Sr., John WHITEHEAD.

7DB259   21 May 1751:   Inventory of the estate
of William PURDY by Evan PURDY and William PURDY.

7DB260   21 Mar 1751:   Lemuel BOUSH to Samuel
BOUSH for 5 lbs. 600 acres - same land Col. Maximillian BOUSH the Elder father to Samuel and grandfather to Lemuel bought of Morris FITZGERALD. Wit:
Anthony LAWSON, James HOLT, John HAMILTON.

7DB266   16 Jul 1751:   Inventory of the estate
of Smith SHEPARD by Frances SHEPARD.

7DB266   16 Jul 1751:   Inventory of the estate
of Richard DROUT.

7DB267   20 Aug 1751:   Appraisal of the estate
of Michael SHERWOOD by Tully WILLIAMSON, Henry WHITE,
James MOORE, John BONNEY.

7DB270   2 Oct 1751/15 Oct 1741:   Elinor BUCHANAN
- my children. Ex: Christen WRIGHT. Wit: John HAR-
PER, Anne NORRIS, Sarah SNAILE, Susanah MOORE.

7DB278   16 Feb 1750/1/20 Nov 1751:   Richard
GARNOR - wife Elizabeth, son Adam, three children.
Ex: wife and son-in-law William CONSAUL. Wit: Henry
BURGESS, Francis BURGESS.

7DB279   19 Nov 1751:   Cornelius CALVERT, Mariner
of Norfolk Co and wife Elizabeth (one of daughters
and coheirs of John THOROWGOOD, Sr.) to Dr. Chris-
topher WRIGHT for 5 shillings half of 705 acres where
John THOROWGOOD, Sr. lived - other half to William
KEELING and wife Mary, other daughter of said THOROW-
GOOD. Wit: Robert DICKSON, Anthony LAWSON, George
WISHART, Thomas WISHART.

7DB281   19 Nov 1751:   Audit of the estate of
Thomas HILL by Joel CORNICK, Lemuel CORNICK.

7DB281   19 Nov 1751:   Appraisal of the estate
of James GISBORN by Adam TOOLY, Robert READE, Lawrence DOYLEY.

7DB288   19 Nov 1751:   Inventory of the estate
of Peter ELLET by Robert PATERSON, Joel CORNICK.

7DB290   17 Dec 1751:   David VALLENTINE and wife
Frances (one of five sisters and coheirs of Thomas
COCKROFT) to William TAYLOR for 5 shillings their
fifth of 138 acres. Wit: William HARPER, Jeremiah
PETREE.

7DB292   17 Dec 1751:   Daniel HUTCHINGS, mariner
of Norfolk to Robert MOSELEY fo5 5 shillings 102
acres which Nathaniel HUTCHINGS father of Daniel
purchased of John HUTCHINGS. Wit: Anthony LAWSON,
Gershom NIMMO, William TAYLOR.

7DB295   21 Jan 1752:   William JACOB to John
son of Charles HENLEY for 90 lbs. 165 acres. Wit:
_____ HUTCHINGS, John BIDDLE, William ROBINSON.

7DB297   17 Jan 1752:   Audit of the estate of
Joseph HARMON by Arthur SAYER.

7DB301   18 Feb 1752:   Appraisal of the estate
of John WILBUR by Simon WHITEHURST, Richard LAND.

7DB303   21 Jan 1751/18 Feb 1742:   Lancaster
LOVETT, Sr. - son John, wife Aliff. Ex: William
son of William KEELING. Wit: William KEELING, Sr.,
William WOODHOUSE.

7DB305   5 Feb 1752/18 Feb 1752:   William MALBONE
- cozen William MOSELEY son of Maj. Francis MOSELEY,
Francis LAND, all the children of my uncle Maj Francis MOSELEY. Ex: Francis LAND, cozen William MOSE-
LEY. Wit: Jacob ELLEGOOD, Mary RICE.

7DB307   17 Mar 1752:   James DAUGE deed of gift
to brother Richard DAUGE 45 acres, part of a plantation our father William divided in the presence of
Peter MALBONE and Cornelius HENLEY. Wit: John BON-
NEY, Sr., Cornelius HENLEY.

7DB307   24 Jul 1749/19 Feb 1752:   Robert BURLEY
- wife Martha, daughter Susanah, brother-in-law Lemuel WHITEHURST. Wit: William GODFREY.

7DB307   17 Mar 1752:   William KEELING, Jr. and
wife Mary and Cornelius CALVERT and wife Elizabeth
to Lemuel CARTWRIGHT for 5 shillings 50 acres - same
land John THOROWGOOD father of Mary and Elizabeth
died seized of. Wit: Adam KEELING, Jr., James CAR-
RAWAY, Robert CARTWRIGHT, William CARROWAY.

7DB311   17 Mar 1752:   Inventory of the estate
of William DAUGE by John BONNEY, Sr. Tully WILLIAM-
SON, Cornelius HENLEY.

7DB314   3 Oct 1749/17 Mar 1752:   Peter MALBONE
- sons James, Jonathan, Phillip, Peter, Malicha,
Solomon and John, wife Mary. Ex: wife and son James.
Wit: Cornelius HENDLEY, Edward BONNEY, Jr., John
BONNEY, Sr.

7DB319 17 Mar 1752: John WHIDDON of Norfolk Co deed of gift to godson John CAWSON son of Jonas CAWSON. Wit: William PORTLOCK, Christopher CAWSON.

7DB319 17 Mar 1752: Audit of the estate of John WILBUR by James KEMPE, Tully ROBINSON.

7DB323 21 Apr 1752: Inventory of the estate of Peter MALBONE.

7DB324 20 May 1752: Richard DUDLEY and wife Mary daughter of Capt. Tully SMYTH, dec. to John DUDLEY for 6 shillings 140 acres, same land Richard DUDLEY the Elder father of said DUDLEY exchanged with Charles SMYTH. Wit: Benjamin MOSELEY, Thomas WILLIAMSON.

7DB327 19 May 1752: Samuel SMYTH attorney of Capt. Thomas QUAY to Tully MOSELEY for 5 shillings 50 acres called Edmonds New Survey, same land Tully EMPEROR grandfather of Tully MOSELEY left to his grandson Thomas MOSELEY and by right of heirship George MOSELEY sold to Thomas QUAY. Wit: Peter DALE, Anthony WALKE, Jr., Jonathan SAUNDERS.

7DB328 19 May 1752: Appraisal of the estate of Richard GARDNER by Joel CORNICK, Lemuel CORNICK.

7DB330 28 Apr 1752/16 Jun 1752: William FENTRESS, Sr. - wife Mary, sons Samuel, Thomas and Anthony; daughters Martha, Ann BALLENTINE, Liddy and Mary; grandchildren William, Mary and James VILLARY. Ex: son Anthony. Wit: Thomas WILES, Abraham WILLEROY, Jemima FENTRESS.

7DB331 16 Jun 1752: Inventory of the estate of Philip WOODHOUSE by Lemuel CORNICK, William WOODHOUSE.

7DB332 16 Jan 1752: Audit of the estate of William LOVETT by Joel CORNICK, William WOODHOUSE, John KEELING.

7DB333 21 Jul 1752: James SMYTH to James HUNTER for 5 shillings 120 acres on the Western Shore - same land which George SMITH, dec. devised by his last will to John SMYTH, dec. father of the said James. Wit: Thomas LAWSON, Samuel FENTRISS, Arthur SAYER.

7DB338 22 Jul 1752: William TAYLOR to William HARPER for 5 shillings 50 acres which Jehue COCKROFT dec. grandfather of said TAYLOR purchased on Little Creek.

7DB342 21 Jul 1752: Inventory of the estate of Lancaster LOVETT by William WOODHOUSE, Charles HILL.

7DB343 26 Sep 1752: William STIBBINS and wife Elizabeth to John CANN for 5 shillings 260 acres - part of a larger tract given by the last will of Adam KEELING, father of Elizabeth. Wit: James HOLT, John TERRY, Joseph MITCHEL.

7DB347 26 Sep 1752: William LANGLEY to Capt.
James IVY for 160 lbs. 250 acres on the Eastern
Shore given LANGLEY by the will of Jeremiah LANG-
LEY. Wit: George COLLINGS, John WEBLIN, Hugh PURDY,
L. CONNER.

7DB352 26 Sep 1752: Inventory of the estate
of Samuel POWERS by James ASHLEY, Mary POWER.

7DB356 26 Sep 1752: Audit of Isaac WHITE by
Lemuel CORNICK, William WOODHOUSE.

7DB367 5 Dec 1751/26 Sep 1752: James LANGLEY
- wife Sarah, daughter Anna wife of Dr. George ROU-
VIERE, daughter Frances, son-in-law Dr. George ROU-
VIERE. Ex: wife. Wit: William NIMMO, James ASHLEY,
Amy POWERS.

7DB371 17 Oct 1752: Audit of the estate of
James JONES by Thomas WISHART, James ASHLEY, Thurmur HOGGARD.

7DB391 19 Oct 1752/21 Nov 1752: John MUNDEN
the Elder - sons John, Aquilla and Stephen, Mary
WHICHARD, daughter James LEGGET, grandson John BROCK.
Ex: son John. Wit: Joel CORNICK, Robert HOLMES,
Mary WHICHARD.

7DB393 19 Dec 1752: George WISHART to Moses
FENTRISS son of John FENTRISS, Sr., dec. for 5 shil-
lings 50 acres. Wit: Thomas WALKE, Lemuel CARTWRIGHT,
Benjamin MOSELEY.

7DB401 17 Nov 1752/19 Dec 1752: John DORY -
wife, two children. Ex: wife and Arthur SAYER.
Wit: Thomas WALKE, William JACOB, Adam LOVETT.

7DB402 19 Dec 1752: Appraisal of the estate
of John MUNDEN by Joel CORNICK, William KEELING,
Sr., Lemuel CORNICK.

7DB408 16 Jan 1753: Richard BONNEY, dec. bequeathed to wife Margarett WHITEHURST 133 acres who
sells it to Edward BONNEY for 2 lbs. Wit: Cason
MOORE, John POWER.

7DB409 24 Oct 1752/17 Jan 1753: Samuel HOLMES
- sons John and Samuel, wife Sarah, daughters Dinah
JONES, Elizabeth and Francis. Ex: wife and son John.
Wit: Thomas CONE, James HOLMES, Henry HOLMES.

7DB410 16 Jan 1753: Inventory of the estate
of William FENTRISS by Anthony FENTRISS.

7DB420 20 Mar 1753: William WARD and wife
Margrett to Jacob MOORE for 6 shillings 25 acres
of marsh - being half of land Margret bought of her
father Charles KELLEY, Sr. Wit: Edward CAPPS, Sr.,
Nathan BONNEY, Cason MOORE.

7DB424 20 Mar 1753: Moses FENTRISS, Sr. and
son Lemuel for 5 shillings 50 acres to son Aaron
near the Cypress Swamp. Wit: Thomas WALKE, John
ACKISS, Henry LAMOUNT, Jr.

7DB430   3 Mar 1753/20 Mar 1753:   William KEELING
the Elder - sons William, John and Henry; daughters
Frances SMITH, Elizabeth THOROWGOOD, Mary, Margret
and Anna; grandsons William and Argyl THOROWGOOD,
wife Amy. Ex: son William. Wit: William CROMPTON,
William COX, Alexander KEELING.

7DB431   17 Jan 1753/20 Mar 1753:   Robert MAR-
TINDALE - James PASTEURS of Norfolk Co, brothers
and sisters John MARTINDALE at Cape Fear NC, William MARTINDALE, Elizabeth TODD, Jeane BARNS and
Mary SAUL of Cumberland, England. Ex: Edward Hack
MOSELEY. Wit: Robert DICKSON, William HANCOCK, Anthony LAWSON.

7DB432   2 Feb 1753/20 Mar 1753:   Elizabeth GIS-
BORN - daughter Prudence LEGET, son James SIMMONS,
Providence SIMMONS, heir of daughter Mary ETHREDGE,
daughters Ann MILLER and Elizabeth LEGGET, son Jo-
seph CORBELE, grandson James SIMMONS. Ex: son John.
Wit: Benjamin COMINGS, James TOOLY, Elizabeth COMINGS.

7DB432   20 Mar 1753:   Appraisal of the estate
of John BALL by Henry MATTHIAS, William SALMON, James
SMYTH.

7DB433   6 Feb 1753/20 Mar 1753:   Eve ETHEREDGE
- sons Anthony and David, grandson Richard, daughter-in-law Mary ETHEREDGE, daughter Amy BALLONS,
granddaughter Elizabeth ETHEREDGE. Ex: son Anthony.
Wit: Henry JAMESON, Ann BALL, Ann ETHEREDGE.

7DB433   1 Apr 1747/20 Mar 1753:   Francis SOREY
- sons Andrew and William, daughters Sedey and Dina,
wife Ann. Ex: wife and son Andrew. Wit: Jacob
BARBER, James ETHEREDGE, Prudance BARBER.

7DB434   20 Mar 1753:   Inventory of the estate
of Samuel HOLMES by Thomas CONE, John CHAPMAN, Tully
R. SMITH.

7DB434   20 Mar 1753:   Appraisal of the estate
of Batson WHITEHURST by Thomas WALKE, William CON-
SAUL, Job GASKING, Jr.

7DB435   20 Mar 1753:   Inventory of the estate
of Edmond ABSALOM by Simon WHITEHURST, Francis CLARKE,
Arthur WHITEHURST.

7DB435   26 Jan 1753/20 Mar 1753:   James HAYNES
- wife and two children. Ex: wife. Wit: Lemuel
CORNICK, Erasmus HAYNES, William SILLAVEN.

7DB436   ---/12 Mar 1753:   Elizabeth MONGOMRE -
noncupative will - son John. Wit: Burroughs MOSE-
LEY, Elizabeth WIGGIN.

7DB436   24 Jan 1753/20 Mar 1753:   Henry HOLMES
- brothers James and John, daughters Elizabeth and
Tamer. Ex: brother James and John CHAPMAN. Wit:
Thomas CONE, James HOLMES, John CHAPMAN.

7DB447   22 Mar 1753/17 Apr 1753:   Jacob ELLE-
GOOD - three daughters Ann, Margritt and Rebecca,
William ACHESON and wife Rebeccah, son Jacob, wife
Ann. Ex: wife. Wit: William KEELING, Job GASKING,
Solomon WILKINS.

7DB448 19 Mar 1753/17 Apr 1753: James NIMMO, Sr. - wife Mary; sons William, Gershom, Jacob and James; daughter Jennet. Ex: sons William and Gershom. Wit: George ROUVIERE, Jacob HUNTER, John HARPER.

7DB439 28 Feb 1753/17 Apr 1753: John HUNTER, Sr. - wife Jacomine; sons Jacob, John, Thomas and James; daughters Margaret HARPER, Mary CARTWRIGHT, Jacomine, Pemmy and Joyce. Ex: wife. Wit: Dinah WILLIAMSON, Amy BARROT, Arthur SAYER.

7DB450 6 Mar 1753/17 Apr 1753: John BATTEN - John BONNEY, daughter Dinah MASON, son George, daughters Mary and Sarah, wife Mary. Ex: son George and daughter Dinah MASON. Wit: Tully WILLIAMSON, John HEATH.

7DB451 3 Mar 1752/17 Apr 1753: William MORRIS - wife Elizabeth, sons William, Thomas, Josiah, Arthur, Francis and James. Ex: wife and sons William and Thomas. Wit: James NIMMO, Josias MORRIS, Jr., James ALDERSON.

7DB452 15 Feb 1753/17 Apr 1753: William OAKHAM - sons William, John and Willaby, daughter Isabell____, wife Sarah, daughters Sarah and Mary. Ex: wife. Wit: William SENECA, George BOOTH, John BATTEN.

7DB453 5 Mar 1753/17 Apr 1753: Erasmus HAYNES - sons Erasmus, Joel, Joshua, William, Thomas, Henry and Francis and son Jeam's child. Ex: son Erasmus. Wit: Frances CORNICK, John WHITEHEAD, Sr., John BONNEY, Sr.

7DB434 2 Apr 1753/17 Apr 1753: John GRIFFIN - son John; daughters Elizabeth, Mary, Frances and Sarah; daughter Ruth BROWN and her son Moses. Ex: wife and son John. Wit: Thomas WHITEHURST, John POWER.

7DB455 8 Apr 1753/17 Apr 1753: John DUDLEY - son Richard, brother Daniel, father-in-law William CARTWRIGHT, wife Margret. Ex: father-in-law. Wit: John FLINCH, Daniel DUDLEY, Robert BURROUGH.

7DB455 31 Mar 1753: Appraisal of the estate of James PETREE by Anthony MOSELEY, James HUNTER.

7DB456 17 Apr 1753: Inventory of the estate of Anthony WHITEHURST by Moses ROBERTS, John ASHBY, John JAMES.

7DB455 17 Apr 1753: Inventory of the estate of Elizabeth MONTGOMERY by Anthony MOSELEY, James HUNTER.

7DB459 15 May 1753: Charles GASKING to Lemuel GASKING 200 acres in exchange for 150 acres. Wit: Samuel TENANT, James MOORE, Jr., James CARRAWAY.

7DB463 15 May 1753: Inventory of the estate of William MALBONE by Thomas WALKE, George WISHART, John INCE, Jr.

7DB467   27 Apr 1751/15 May 1753:   Anne BLAIR -
son John SIMMONS, daughter Betty HERBERT,son William
SIMMONS, cousens Thomas and John HERBERT. Ex: Adam
TOOLY and Southwood SIMMONS. Wit: Hillary KEATON,
George HEWITT, Andrew BRAN.

7DB468   15 May 1753:   Inventory of the estate
of Elizabeth GISBORN.

7DB468   15 May 1753:   Appraisal of the estate
of William MORRIS by Dennis DAULEY, Tully WILLIAM-
SON, Henry WHITE, John WHITEHEAD.

7DB469   15 May 1753:   Inventory of the estate
of Edward BROWN by John BONNEY, Sr. Tully WILLIAM-
SON, Cornelius HENDLEY.

7DB469   1 May1753:   Audit of Moses BALL by
Thomas WALKE, Francis T. LAND, Samuel TENANT.

7DB470   16 May 1753:   Appraisal of the estate
of Robert MARTINDALE by Nathaniel MCCLENAHAN, William ROBINSON, William HANCOCK.

7DB470   15 May 1753:   Inventory of the estate
of John BATTEN.

7DB471   15 May 1753:   Audit of the estate of
John MUNDEN by Joel CORNICK, William WOODHOUSE, John
KEELING.

7DB471   15 May 1753:   Inventory of the estate
of William OAKHAM by John RUSSEL, James MAJOR.

7DB471   15 May 1753:   Appraisal of the estate
of John GWIN by John GORNTO, Jr., William WOODHOUSE,
Sr., Francis WOODHOUSE.

7DB472   29 Apr 1753? Appraisal of the estate
of William JACOB by Thomas WALKE, James KEMPE, George
WISHART.

7DB474   20 May 1753/19 Jun 1753:   William CART-
WRIGHT - wife Mary, Robert, grandson William, daugh-
ters Elizabeth HARPER, Margaret DUDLEY, Martha CARRA-
WAY, Frances, Anne, Sarah and Amy. Ex: wife and son
Robert. Wit: James CARROWAY, Lewis PRICE, William
HOLMES.

7DB475   27 Dec 1752/19 Jun 1753:   George BEARRY
- sons John, Thomas, George and Richard, wife Sarah.
Ex: sons Thomas and John. Wit: John RUSSELL, John
COATES, Edward CAPPS.

7DB476   19 Dec 1751/19 Jun 1753:   William BENSON
- Betty DALE, Marian wife of John KEELING, Rachel
DALE, sister Elizabeth DALE. Ex: sister. Wit: Lem-
uel CORNICK, Francis CORNICK, Thomas KEELING, Jr.

7DB476   22 Feb 1753/19 Jun 1753:   Robert MASON
- son James, daughter Betty, wife Mary. Ex: wife
and son. Wit: John RUSSEL, John BATTEN, Francis
SHIP.

7DB477   11 Dec 1753/19 Jun 1753:   William COR-
NICK - sons John and Nathan, daughter Elizabeth,
wife Betty. Ex: wife. Wit: John RUSSEL, John MORSE,
John WHITEHEAD, Sr.

7DB478   10 Oct 1752/19 Jun 1753:   John CAPPS -
sons James, Hillary, John, Solomon and Charles; daughters Mary, Margrett and Amy; wife Dina. Ex: wife and
Solomon WHITEHURST. Wit: Charles HARTHY(?), Cason
MOORE.

7DB479   25 Dec 1752/19 Jun 1753:   Cornelius
HENLEY - son James, daughters Kezia MOORE, Mary
and Elizabeth, wife Nowdina. Ex: wife and son-in-
law Cason MOORE. Wit: John FENTROUS, Moses MECLALIN.

7DB480   10 Mar 1753/19 Jun 1753:   Solomon CEATON
- sons James, John, Hillary and Thomas, daughter
Sarah. Ex: sons John and Hillery. Wit: Samuel
CREEKMAN, Francis ETHEREDGE, Edmond CREEKMAN.

7DB481   19 Jun 1753:   Appraisal of Benjamin
MOSELEY by James HUNTER, Christopher MOSELEY, William MOSELEY.

7DB482   19 Jun 1753:   Inventory of the estate
of John HUNTER by Jacamine HUNTER.

7DB483   20 Jun 1753:   Inventory of the estate
of Thomas LAWSON by Thomas WISHART, William DENNY,
Robert MOSELEY.

7DB483   19 Jun 1753:   Inventory of the estate
of Robert HOLMES by Edward CANNON, Joel CORNICK,
William WOODHOUSE.

7DB484   19 Jun 1753:   Appraisal of the estate
of Elizabeth WILBUR by Simon WHITEHURST, James LOVETT,
Robert MURDEN.

7DB484   19 Jun 1753:   Inventory of the estate
of John BUSKY by Joel CORNICK, William WOODHOUSE,
John MUNDEN.

7DB485   19 Jun 1753:   Inventory of the estate
of John GRIFFIN by John BONNEY, Sr., Tully WILLIAM-
SON, Cornelius HENLEY.

7DB485   19 Jun 1753:   Inventory of the estate
of William CONSAUL, Jr. by Edward CANNON, Adam KEE-
LING, Battson WHITEHURST.

7DB490   3 May 1753/17 Jul 1753:   Tully ROBIN-
SON SMYTH - three daughters Elizabeth Frances and
Susanah, mother, wife Francis. Ex: wife and Wil-
liam KEELING. Wit: George ROUVIERE, William KEEL-
ING.

7DB491   17 Jul 1753:   Appraisal of the estate
of Mark ROBARDS by William WOODHOUSE, Joel CORNICK,
Henry CORNICK.

7DB491   17 Jul 1753:   Inventory of the estate
of James HAYNES by Joel CORNICK, William CONSAUL,
Alexander POOLE

7DB492   26 Mar 1753/17 Jul 1753:   Kiteley ROE -
wife Mary, daughter Eleanor PHILLIPS, brother Robert,
Sarah wife of Benjamin COMMING, John, James and William sons of Sophia FENTRISS, Faney FENTRISS, Kiteley ROE son of Robert. Ex: wife and Benjamin BALL.
Wit: John CARTEE, William WILLIAMS, Michael FLING.

7DB494   17 Jul 1753:   Inventory of William COR-
NICK by John BONNEY, Dennis DAWLEY, Tully WILLIAMSON.

7DB495   18 Jul 1753:   Appraisal of the estate
of Patrick BROOKS by Nathaniel MCCLENAHAN, George
JAMESON, Edward DENBY.

7DB496   17 Jul 1753:   Inventory of the estate
of George BERRY, Sr. by Thomas BERRY, John BERRY,
Jr.

7DB497   17 Jul 1753:   Audit of the estate of
Ales CLARK by George WISHART, Thomas WISHART.

7DB502   21 Aug 1753:   Capt. William ELLEGOOD to
Thomas HUNTER for 100 lbs. land in Little Creek heired
from father John. Wit: Thomas WALKE, Anthony LAWSON,
Thomas WISHART, William HUNTER.

7DB507   22 Aug 1753:   Josiah MORRIS deed of gift
to sons Josiah, Willis and Willoughby 200 acres at
Nanney's Creek. Wit: Thomas WALKE, William MORRIS,
Thomas MORRIS.

7DB508   21 Aug 1753:   Sarah JACOB deed of gift
to son Isaac. Wit: Anthony MOSELEY, Arthur SAYER.

7DB509   21 Aug 1753:   Sarah JACOB deed of gift
to daughter Rebecca. Wit: Anthony MOSELEY, Arthur
SAYER.

7DB509   14 Feb 1752:   John SHARWOOD, Sr. - sons
James, Josiah and John, daughters Sarah, Mary and
Ollive. Ex: wife Mary. Wit: John JAMES, John CAPPS.

7DB510   3 Jan 1752/21 Aug 1753:   George CAPPS -
sons George and William, wife Sarah, daughter Pembrook. Ex: wife. Wit: Solomon WILLIAMS, Richard
CAPPS.

7DB512   21 Aug 1753:   Appraisal of the estate
of Kiteley ROE by Thomas OLD, Robert REED, Adam
TOOLY.

7DB512   21 Aug 1753:   Appraisal of the estate
of Anne BLAIR by John WHITEHEAD, James MOORE, Richard LESTER.

7DB512   21 Aug 1753:   Appraisal of the estate
of Dorcas LESTER by James MOORE, Richard LESTER,
James KING.

7DB516   18 Sep 1753:   John LAMOUNT deed of
gift to children Arthur, Thomas, Cornelius, Elizabeth and Lydia. Wit: Robert PATTERSON, Robert BUR-
FOOT, Kezia CONSAUL.

7DB518   18 Sep 1753:   Inventory of the estate
of George CAPPS by Sarah CAPPS.

7DB519   18 Sep 1753:   Appraisal of the estate
of Erasmus HAYNES by John BONNEY, Sr., Tully WIL-
LIAMSON, John WHITEHEAD, Henry WHITE.

7DB519   18 Sep 1753:   Appraisal of the estate
of Tully R. SMYTH by James CAWSON, George JAMIESON,
John INCE, Jr.

7DB520   19 Sep 1753:   Appraisal of the estate
of Adam ACKISS by William WEST, Simon WHITEHURST,
Arthur WHITEHURST.

7DB520   16 Oct 1753:   Appraisal of the estate
of Capt. William KEELING by Lemuel CORNICK, Charles
HILL, William WOODHOUSE.

7DB521   16 Oct 1753:   John PRESCOTE of Norfolk
Co deed of gift to son-in-law Anthony ETHEREDGE.
Wit: Thomas GRAINGER, Sarah NICHOLAS, Dinah MATTHIAS.

7DB521   16 Oct 1753:   Appraisal of the estate
of Henry HOLMES by Thomas WISHART, William HUNTER,
Thurmur HOGGARD.

7DB522   16 Oct 1753:   Inventory of the estate
of Solomon CATEN.

7DB523   20 Nov 1753:   John ACKISS to Anthony
WALKE, Jr. for 5 shillings 99 acres called Possum
Quarter that John ACKISS, dec. left to his son Fran-
cis, dec. who left it to his son John. Wit: Thomas
Reynolds WALKER, John FLINCH, Anthony ETHERIDGE,
Jonathan WHITEHURST, Charles MORRIS, Francis WILLIAM-
SON.

7DB527   20 Nov 1753:   William KEELING Ex of
Lancaster LOVETT to David MCCLENAHAN for 13 lbs 10
shillings 100 acres in the Western Shore swamp which
belonged to John LOVETT, dec. father to said Lancaster who left it by his will to his son William who
died without issue and so it descended to Lancaster.
Wit: Nathaniel MCCLENAHAN, Jonathan SAUNDERS, Maximillian BOUSH.

7DB529   20 Nov 1753:   Joseph WALSTONE and wife
Mary to Henry BURGESS for 6 shillings 50 acres known
as CREEDLES left to Mary by her father Richard GARNOR.
Wit: Anthony LAWSON, John ACKISS, Jacob HUNTER, Francis LAND son of Renatus LAND.

7DB532   20 Nov 1753:   Godfrey MALBONE deed of
gift to cousin Francis MALBONE 200 acres which he
received as heir of William MALBONE. Wit: James
DAWSON, Robert MELVIN, Henry LAMOUNT, Michael HACKETT.

7DB533   21 Nov 1753:   Mary KNOWIS wife of John
deed of gift to children James SMYTH, Mary WHITEHURST,
Amy SMYTH, Elizabeth SMYTH, Keziah SMYTH and Frances.
Wit: Thomas WALKE, John WHITEHURST, Francis T. LAND,
John ACKISS, Francis WISHART.

7DB533   20 Nov 1753:   Audit of the estate of
Richard GARNOR by Joel CORNICK, John BUSKY, Alexander POOLE.

7DB535   8 Nov 1753/20 Nov 1753:   Job GASKING -
sons Job, Charles, Lemuel, Henry and Jacob; daughters Rebecca and Sarah; son-in-law John KEELING.
Ex: sons Job and Charles. Wit: Adam KEELING, Martha KEELING, Mary WHITE.

7DB536   11 Mar 1752/20 Nov 1753:   John RAINEY -
sons John and Thomas; daughters Mary, Betty, Amy
and Anney. Ex: John BONNEY, Jr., Morris HILL. Wit:
John DEARMORE, Jean DEARMORE, Cason MOORE.

7DB541   18 Dec 1753:   James HUNTER to daughter
Elizabeth and son-in-law Samuel TENANT deed of gift
of 400 acres on the South side of the Eastern Branch.
Wit: William HUNTER, William MOSELEY, Anthony BURROUGH.

7DB542   18 Dec 1753:   Appraisal of the estate of
Francis SOREY by Thomas OLD, Samuel SMITH, James RAN-
DOLPH.

7DB544   28 Oct 1749/18 Dec 1753:   Thomas ELK -
wife Elizabeth.   Ex: wife.   Wit: Robert READ, Edmond
DOD, Richard TENTHON(?), George HEWITT.

7DB547   11 May 1753/18 Dec 1753:   James MOORE -
daughter Ann TATEM, sons James, John and Francis.
Ex: son James and William NIMMO.   Wit: Thomas GRAIN-
GER, James GODFREY, John CHAPMAN.

7DB549   18 Dec 1753:   Appraisal of the estate
of Dinah WILLIAMSON by Samuel BOUSH, Jacob HUNTER,
John HARPER.

7DB549   18 Dec 1753:   Appraisal of the estate
of William FRANKLIN.

7DB550   18 Dec 1753:   Audit of the estate of
William CONSAUL by Lemuel CORNICK, Alexander POOLE.

7DB552   15 Jan 1754:   Dinah BONNEY deed of gift
to daughter Frankey 50 acres near the Cypress Swamp.
Wit: Morris HILL, John DEARMORE

7DB553   15 Jan 1754:   Audit of the estate of
Margaret ELLEGOOD.

7DB554   18 Nov 1753/15 Jan 1754:   Charles WHITE-
HURST - wife Mary, sons William and Charles, daugh-
ter Amy, all my children.   Ex: son John and Arthur
WHITEHURST.   Wit: Thomas ROBINSON, Dennis DAULEY.

7DB555   15 Jan 1754:   Appraisal of the estate
of William CARTWRIGHT by Francis T. LAND, John BIDDLE'
Adam LOVETT.

7DB555   15 Jan 1754:   Audit of the estate of
William WEBLIN by Lemuel CORNICK, William KEELING,
John KEELING.

7DB556   19 Feb 1754:   Charles JAMES to William
JAMES for 5 shillings 100 acres - land of Edward
JAMES, dec.   Wit: Lemuel CORNICK, Thorowgood KEE-
LING, John HAYNES.

7DB564   18 Feb 1754:   James WHITEHURST, ship-
wright to Thomas son of Thomas WHITEHURST for 5 shillings 50 acres at the head of the Eastern Branch -
land left him by his father Thomas WHITEHURST the
Elder.   Wit: Nathaniel MCCLENAHAN, Jacob HUNTER,
James ASHLEY.

7DB576   19 Feb 1754:   Appraisal of the estate
of Job GASKING by Lemuel CORNICK, William WOODHOUSE,
George WEBLIN.

7DB577   19 Feb 1754:   Audit of the estate of
William LOVETT by Lemuel CORNICK, William KEELING,
William WOODHOUSE.

7DB580 16 Apr 1754: Anthony and Charles Lawson to Elias CORNISH of Curratuck NC for 5 shillings 150 acres near Back Bay which their father Thomas left them. and their brother Thomas who is since dead. Wit: Francis WILLIAMSON, Thomas WALKE, William NIMMO.

7DB587 21 Aug 1753/16 Apr 1754: Robert HUG-GINS - sons Robert, Natt and Markham, daughters Olive, Argent and Mary, grandson William CARTWRIGHT, wife Mary. Ex: wife. Wit: John SHIPP, Thomas GRAIN-GER, Dinah GRAINGER.

7DB589 5 Oct 1752/16 Apr 1754: John GORNTO - sons Arthur and John, daughters Frances, Elizabeth, Amy, Lidia and Margret HENDLEY. Ex: sons John and Arthur. Wit: John HAYNES, Mary HENLEY, William WOODHOUSE.

7DB590 18 Jan 1754/16 Apr 1754: Joel CORNICK - sons Joel, William and Henry, wife. Ex: wife and Lemuel CORNICK. Wit: Henry CORNICK, Elizabeth FON-TAINE, Margret BROCK

7DB511 9 Jan 1752/16 Apr 1754: Richard SMITH - Holsterd HOLEWELL, mother, coson Richard HEATH, sis-ters Sarah LEETIH, Elizabeth, Mary and Lidia. Ex: Solomon HEATH. Wit: John GISBURN, Jacobus HEATH.

7DB592 6 Feb 1753/16 Apr 1754: Christopher PHILPOT, daughter Elizabeth, Rachel WEST, wife Mary. Ex: wife. Wit: Gilburd JAMES, Elizabeth SMITH, Richard SMITH.

7DB592 12 Aug 1752/16 Apr 1754: Worsell AL-DERSON - son John, wife, all my children. Ex: Ar-thur SAYER. Wit: John NAYLES, Sarah NAYLES.

7DB593 17 Apr 1754: Frances BROWN relict of Edward BROWN deed of gift to daughter Elizabeth and her husband Morris HILL. Wit: John BONNEY, Jr. Wil-loughby AIRS, Luke HILL.

7DB593 16 Apr 1754: Audit of the estate of Dinah WILLIAMSON by Thomas WALKE, James KEMPE, Sam-uel TENANT.

7DB594 16 Apr 1754: Inventory of the estate of Charles WHITEHURST by Dennis DAULEY, Henry DAU-LEY, Thomas MOORE.

7DB594 21 May 1754: John MERCER of Norfolk Co and wife Martha and Frances CONDON of Norfolk to William AITCHESON, Merchant of Norfolk Co for 5 shillings 180 acres which belonged to Capt James CONDON who died intestate and it descended to five sisters - Elizabeth late wife of William STEVENSON, Jane who married Elias WILLS, Sarah who married John GEMMEL and died and her heirs died, said Mar-tha and Frances. Wit: Josiah SMYTH, George ABYVON, A. WHITE, James HOLT.

7DB598 21 May 1754: John and Richard SCOTT to Simon WHITEHURST for 25 lbs. 220 acres - part of Thomas SCOTT'S patent. Wit: Thomas KEELING, Edward DENBY, James MOORE·

7DB600   22 May 1754:   Agreement between Joseph
BELL of NC and Mary FAZACKERLY - Mary's grandfather
Richard CORBETT left property to daughters Abigail
who married Thomas FAZACKERLY and Mary who married
Joseph BELL - division of property.

7DB611   21 May 1754:   Inventory of the estate
of James BANNISTER by Lemuel CORNICK, John KEELING,
Henry LAMOUNT.

7DB612   22 May 1754:   Audit of the estate of
Richard MOY by Edward DENBY, George JAMISON, George
OLDNER.

7DB612   22 Apr 1754/21 May 1754:   Michel FEN-
TRISS - daughter Keziah, son John, wife Elizabeth,
granddaughter Amy WHITEHURST. Ex: wife and Moses
FENTRISS. Wit: Thomas GRAINGER, Nathaniel NICHOLAS,
Matthew MATTHIAS.

7DB613   4 May 1754/21 May 1754:   Malacai NICHOL-
SON - brother William, sister Prudence WILSON, Dinah
OLDNER, Elizabeth HUCHANS and Anne CHILLIS. Ex:
George OLDNER. Wit: Edward LATIMER, Josiah WILSON,
Lemuel LANGLEY.

7DB614   21 May 1754:   Appraisal of the estate
of Worsell ALDERSON by Tully WILLIAMSON, William
CARREL, Josias MORRIS.

7DB614   21 May 1754:   Appraisal of the estate
of John GORNTO by John HAYNES, William WOODHOUSE,
Henry WOODHOUSE.

7DB615   13 Dec 1742/21 May 1754:   Andrew NICHO-
LAS - wife, Robert TOOD, merchant. Ex: Robert TODD.
Wit: William WIGGIN, Blandine GALLEY.

7DB615   21 May 1754:   Audit of the estate of
John KAY by Lemuel CORNICK, William KEELING.

7DB616   21 May 1754:   Inventory of the estate
of Thomas ELKS.

7DB624   18 Jun 1754:   Nathaniel NEWTON deed of
gift to daughter Margarette. Wit: Anthony LAWSON

7DB625   18 Jun 1754:   Anthony LAWSON deed of
gift to cousins Anne daughter of Capt. Nathaniel
NEWTON and Charles son of Capt. Arthur SAYER.

7DB625   15 Jun 1754:   Audit of the estate of
Margaret ELLEGOOD relict of Mathew by Anthony WALKE,
James KEMPE, Tully ROBINSON.

7DB626   18 Jun 1754:   Inventory of the estate
of Michael FENTRISS.

7DB627   18 Jun 1754:   Audit of the estate of
Robert HOLMES by Edward CANNON, John KEELING.

7DB627   29 Apr 1754/18 Jun 1754:   William SAL-
MONS - son Willoby, wife. Wit: David FENTRISS,
Lemuel STONE, James CASON.

7DB630   16 Jul 1754:   Anthony ETHERIDGE to Simon
MATTHIAS of Norfolk Co for 5 shillings 33 acres given
him by his mother Eve ETHERIDGE. Wit: Thomas NASH,
Walter SCOTT.

7DB635   16 Jul 1754:   Inventory of the estate
of Capt. Jacob ELLEGOOD by Lemuel CORNICK, William
WOODHOUSE.

7DB635   16 Jul 1754:   Audit of the estate of
John HILL by Thomas WALKE, James KEMPE, George WI-
SHART.

7DB636   16 Jul 1754:   Appraisal of the estate
of John CAPPS by John BONNEY, Sr., Henry DAULEY,
Dennis DAULEY.

7DB636   16 Jul 1754:   Audit of the estate of
Mary DUDLEY by Charles GASKING, John BIDDLE, Adam
LOVETT.

7DB637   16 Jul 1754:   Audit of the estate of
Mark ROBERTS by William KEELING, Alexander POOLE,
Lemuel CORNICK.

7DB639   5 Jun 1754/20 Aug 1754:   Arthur WHITE-
HURST - sons Francis, Arthur, Oden and Tully, wife
Margett, all my children. Ex: wife and Thomas WARD
and Robert WARD. Wit: Thomas WRIGHT, John WHITE-
HURST, Mary WHITEHURST.

7DB640   20 Aug 1754:   Audit of the estate of
John ASHBY by James KEMPE, George WISHART.

7DB640   17 Sep 1754:   Inventory of the estate
of Arthur WHITEHURST by John GORNTO, William WOOD-
HOUSE, Francis WOODHOUSE.

7DB641   17 Sep 1754:   James TOOLY and wife
Betty to William FENTRESS for 6 shillings 100 acres
that John HARBERT bequeathed to his son Thomas and
it descended to Betty as daughter of Thomas. Wit:
Thomas OLD, Henry TRIPPE, Nathaniel NICHOLAS.

7DB643   5 Apr 1753/16 Oct 1754:   John WILLIAM-
SON, Sr. - sons Thomas and John, daughters Priscilla,
Mary MATTHIAS, Sarah MATTHIAS, Sally SHEPHERD. Ex:
son John and daughter Priscilla. Wit: Thomas GRAIN-
GER, John INCE, Sarah RUTLAND.

7DB659   20 Nov 1754:   Inventory of the estate
of Capt. James NIMMO by Samuel BOUSH, Thomas WISHART,
William HUNTER.

7DB660   19 Nov 1754:   Samuel DAVIS of Norfolk
son of Richard DAVIS, ship carpenter to William GOD-
FREY for 40 lbs. 150 acres. Wit: Thomas WALKE, Tully
ROBINSON, Christopher WRIGHT, Andrew STEWART, Joel
SIMMONS.

7DB661   18 May 1754/19 Nov 1754:   Margaret SAYER
- son Arthur, daughter Frances BOUSH, grandchildren
Jonathan SAUNDERS, Margaret MALBONE, Anne and Mar-
garet NEWTON children of daughter Elizabeth, dec.,
Anthony LAWSON, Margarett WALKE, Frances SAYER,
Margaret BOUSH. Ex: son Arthur. Wit: Anthony WALKE,
Elizabeth PARSLEY, Ann MOSELEY.

7DB662   19 Nov 1754:   Inventory of the estate
of John WILLIAMSON, Sr.

7DB663   17 Dec 1754:   Audit of the estate of
Henry AXSTEAD by Thomas WALKE, Francis T. LAND,
James KEMPE.

7DB664 17 Dec 1754: Audit of the estate of
William CARTWRIGHT by Charles GASKINGS, John BID-
DLE, Andrew STEWART.

7DB664 16 Dec 1754: Audit of the estate of
John DUDLEY by Charles GASKING, Adam LOVETT, Andrew
STEWART.

7DB665 17 Dec 1754: Inventory of the estate
of Joel CORNICK by William KEELING, John KEELING,
Jr., William WOODHOUSE, Jr.

7DB665 21 Jan 1755: Robert BURFOOT and wife
Amy to William HOLMES for 7 lbs. land in the Eastern Shore which William CONSAUL died possessed of
and wife Amy now wife of BURFOOT. Wit: Lemuel COR-
NICK, Charles GASKING, Lemuel GASKING.

7DB669 21 Jan 1755: Charles EDWARDS deed of
gift to sons William, Charles, Henry, Solomon and
Obediah, wife Sarah, daughters Frances LAND and
Elizabeth. Wit: John INCE, Jr., Solomon SUGGS,
John STONE.

7DB670 1 May 1754/21 Jan 1755: Ambrose BUR-
FOOT - son Robert, daughter Elizabeth wife of Edward
CANNON, grandson John CANNON, granddaughter Sarah
BURFOOT daughter of daughter Mackie SMYTH wife of
Thomas, daughter Sarah wife of John ABSALOM. Ex:
son Robert. Wit: Margret ELLET, Robert PATERSON.

7DB671 22 Jan 1755: Inventory of the estate
of Robert BURLY by Thomas WILES.

7DB671 21 Jan 1755: Audit of the estate of
Henry BRINSON by James KEMPE, George WISHART, Francis T. LAND

7DB671 22 Jan 1755: Audit of the estate of
Thomas WHITEHURST by William ROBINSON, James KEMPE.

7DB671 18 Feb 1755: William FENTRISS to An-
thony FENTRISS for 5 shillings 100 acres known as
Sambors that father William left him. Wit: Thomas
GRAINGER, Jeremiah MURDEN.

7DB673 18 Feb 1755: Audit of the estate of
William FRANKLIN by John BONNEY, Sr., Tully WILLIAM-
SON, Cason MOORE.

7DB673 13 Apr 1754/18 Feb 1755: Argel THOROW-
GOOD, Sr. - wife Elizabeth son William, daughter
Elizabeth. Ex: wife and Capt. William KEELING her
brother. Wit: Samuel BOUSH, Francis SPRATT, Ann
RICE.

7DB674 15 Apr 1755: Robert LAND son of Edward
to Hezekiah BROWN for 5 shillings 100 acres on Pungo
Rd. Wit: Thomas WALKE, Samuel BOUSH, William HUNTER.

7DB684 15 Apr 1755: Audit of the estate of
John SEALEY by James KEMPE, Thomas WALKE, George
WISHART.

7DB685 20 May 1755: Maximillian BOUSH, Jr.
to Samuel BOUSH for 5 shillings 103 acres left him
by father Maximillian BOUSH, Sr. Wit: James HOLT,
Thomas WALKE, Robert HUGGINS.

7DB698   20 May 1755:   Arthur FRIZZLE to William BIDDLE for 5 shillings 100 acres called Georges left him by his father Daniel. Wit: Thomas WALKE, John ACKISS, John HAYNES, George BALL

7DB700   20May 1755:   Lancaster LOVETT to Joseph WHITE for 5 shillings 239 acres left by his father Lancaster LOVETT. Wit: Thomas KEELING, Gershom NIMMO, John KEELING, Jr.

7DB702   17 Feb 1755/20 May 1755:   Robert THOROWGOOD - wife Blandinah, son Robert. Ex: wife and Thomas KEELING. Wit: Robert BURROUGH, John THOROWGOOD, Sr.

7DB703   21 May 1755:   Audit of the estate of Mary MOORE by Tully ROBINSON, David MCCLENAHAN, William NIMMO.

7DB703   ---/20 May 1755:   Thomas LESTER - noncupative will - wife. Wit: Mary HARPER, Sr., William HARPER, SR.

7DB704   17 Jun 1755:   Inventory of the estate of Richard SANDERLIN by Arthur SAYER.

7DB709   17 Jun 1755:   Elizabeth NICHOLSON deed of gift to children Charles, Betty and Dinah. Wit: William NIMMO, Jr., John HANCOCK, Mary HOLMES.

7DB710   17 Jun 1755:   Appraisal of the estate of Argyl THOROWGOOD by Thomas WISHART, Thomas HAYNES, William HUNTER.

7DB711   17 Jun 1755:   Audit of the estate of William MALBONE by Thomas WALKE, James KEMPE, George WISHART, Samuel TENANT.

7DB711   17 Jun 1755:   Audit of the estate of Henry BRINSON by George WISHART, Francis T. LAND.

7DB712   ---/17 Jan 1755:   John RUSSEL - sons William and John, wife. Ex: wife and John WHITEHAT, Sr. Wit: Tully WILLIAMSON, John GREEN, Dinah MASON.

7DB712   3 Apr 1755/17 Jun 1755:   Nathaniel WHITEHURST - brother Henry. Ex: brother and Thomas WILES. Wit: Thomas WILES, Richard WHITEHURST, James WHITEHURST.

7DB712   17 Jun 1755:   Inventory of the estate of Thomas LESTER by Thomas WISHART, George WISHART, Thomas HAYNES.

7DB714   - Jul 1755:   Inventory of John RUSSEL by Tully WILLIAMSON, James MOORE, Jonathan BONNEY.

7DB714   - Jul 1755:   Appraisal of the estate of Ambrose BURFOOT by Robert PATTERSON, Henry LAMOUNT, Robert JONES.

SURNAME INDEX

ABRAHAM, 19
ABSALOM, 87 104
ABYVON, 101
ACHESON, 94
ACKIS, 57 61
ACKISS, 37 43 45 46 54 61 71 75
    77 88 93 98 99 105
ACKLES, 9
ADAMS, 2 49
AIRES, 6 48 86
AIRS, 59 77 86 101
AITCHESON, 101
ALBRITTON, 41 50 57 66
ALDERSON, 95 101 102
ALGREW, 56
ALLBRITON, 35
ALLEN, 1 14 17 71
ANDERSON, 46
ANGUS, 1-3 5-16 19 29 37
ARTHUR, 1
ASHBEE, 19
ASHBY, 19 26 31 43 66 95 103
ASHLEY, 58 88 90 93 100
ASHLY, 54
ASHWELL, 20
ATTWOOD, 14 24 26 31 34 42 79
ATWOOD, 5 8 38 39 42 47 76
AUSTIN, 80
AVERRY, 3
AVERY, 2 6
AXSTEAD, 59 103
AYERS, 60
BACKER, 33
BAKER, 12 17 21 41 44
BALL, 25 51 74 94 96 97 105
BALLENTINE, 92
BALLONS, 94
BANGER, 79
BANISTER, 55
BANKS, 9 73

BANNISTER, 72 84 102
BARBER, 20 94
BARFOOT, 52 54
BARKER, 8 15
BARLOW, 66 72
BARNES, 57 82
BARNS, 54 57 60 86 94
BARRINGTON, 26 68 69
BARROT, 87 95
BARSLEY, 7 8
BARTEE, 74
BASNETT, 7 23
BASNITT, 11
BATCHELER, 55
BATSON, 89
BATTEN, 95 96
BAX, 49
BEARD, 8
BEARRY, 96
BEARSLEY, 20
BEASHER, 2
BECK, 11 12 18
BECKER, 65
BEDNAM, 5
BEEBURY, 2
BEESLEY, 34
BELL, 23 25 26 35 38 39 85 102
BELLEMY, 46
BELLENY, 15
BENSON, 14 17 18 20 21 38 42
    45 58 62 64 67 76 96
BENTLEY, 58
BENTON, 75
BERRIT, 16
BERRY, 2 12 22 38 47 49 57 63
    69 70 79 98
BIBBERY, 2 25
BIDDLE, 68 69 91 100 103 104
    105
BIDDLES, 50

CARRAWAY,4 16 19 87 91 95 96
CARREL, 66 88 102
CARRILL, 68
CARROWAY, 19 22 25 27 31 32
   35 37 39 44 47 49 50 55 61 73
   83 96
CARRUTHERS, 36
CARTEE, 5 97
CARTWRIGHT, 4 20 26 38 41 57
   61 73 82 83 87 91 93 95 96 10
   101 104
CARY 6 9
CASON, 45 62 66 82 89 102
CATEN, 31 99
CATERELL, 15
CATHRILL, 7 26
CATON, 6 19 20 21
CATTEN, 37
CAVENDER, 84
CAVENER, 11
CAWSON, 67 92 98
CEATON, 97
CHAMNEY, 73
CHAPMAN, 11 15 27 30 35 36 38
   39 55 79 80 86 94 100
CHAPPEL, 12 17 57
CHAPPELL, 23
CHAPPLE, 5
CHAPPLIN, 57
CHEETHAM, 11
CHERRY, 73
CHESHIRE, 50 59 64 77 86 87
CHICHESTER, 44
CHILLIS, 102
CHOICE, 20
CHRISTOPHER, 13
CHURCH, 17 21 24 45
CLARK, 42 49 98
CLARKE, 35 94
CLAY, 82
CLAYDER, 57
CLAYTON, 73
CLOUSE, 39
COATES, 96
COATS, 63
COCKE, 10-12 18-31 34-36 51
COCKIN, 33
COCKROFT, 5 10 15 21 24 25 32
   38 39 43 50-52 55 74 91 92
COCKSIN, 57
COLLINGS, 93

COLLINS, 8 16 18 30 33 56 64 68
   70 77 79
COMINGS, 94
COMINS, 37
COMMING, 97
COMMINGS, 76
CONDON, 16 51 62 73 74 77 81
   84 101
CONE, 93 94
CONNER, 27 41 63 64 72 74 77
   86 93
CONNYER, 71 72
CONSALVO, 52
CONSAUL, 80 84 90 97 98 100
   104
CONSOLBARE, 57
COOK, 44 67
COOPER, 1 2 3 6 11 16 17 18 20
   24 48 49 51 63 90
CORBELE, 94
CORBELL, 53 56 58 59
CORBET, 35 43 53
CORBETT, 12 16 33 40 72 102
CORBITT,9 12 15 22-32 37 40 72
CORNICK, 2 3 6 7 9-12 14 16 18-
   23 25 27 29-31 34 36 40 47
   50-53 55 60 68 72 75 77 79-81
   83 84 86 88-104
CORNISH, 70 101
CORNWALL, 10
CORPEW, 31
CORPREW, 24 45
COTANCO, 49
COTTEN, 25
COTTON, 57 67 69
COWELL, 36
COX, 6 11 34 51 54 59 60 67 69
   74 75 78 79 81 83 85 94
CRAFORD, 9 38
CRAKIN, 82
CRASHLEY, 37 77
CRASHLY, 1
CREED, 7 57 64 65 69 79
CREEDLE, 55
CREEDLES, 99
CREEDS, 63
CREEKMAN, 97
CROMPTON, 33 34 36 37 39 41
   42 43 45 49 76 83 85 94
CROSSLEY, 49
CUDDEL, 39

HARBORD, 17
HARFORD, 2 5 30 74
HARISON, 11 13
HARMON, 67 91
HARPER, 5 10 14 16 25 32 44 45
55 63 70 78 87 89-92 95 96 100
105
HARRIES, 42
HARRISON, 7 12 20 24 26 28 31
53 67 84 89
HARTHY, 97
HARTLEY, 7
HARVAY, 81
HARVEY, 25 26 36 38 50 51 66 76
87
HARYSON, 13
HATTERSLEY, 10 18
HATTERSLY, 14 52
HAWKEY, 51
HAYES, 4-7 11 14 17 23 39 41 49
83 84
HAYNES, 25 30 31 35 51 56 62 64
66-68 72 83 86 88 90 94 95 97
98 100-102 105
HEATH, 5 7 21 24 36 45 46 54-56
78 79 82 95 101
HELDON, 23
HENDLEY, 91 96 101
HENLEY, 7 24 60 63 66 75 79 82
85 91 97 101
HENLY, 8 14 23 58 60 84
HERBERT, 55 96
HERISON, 12 20
HESLETT, 8
HEWETT, 19
HEWITT, 96 100
HICHOLSON, 89
HIDE, 11
HILL, 21 43 75 83 85 89 91 92 99-
101 103
HILLYARD, 1 7-10 23
HILYARD, 51
HODGE, 26
HODGES, 9 69
HOGGARD, 93 99
HOLEWELL, 101
HOLLOWAY, 54
HOLLOWELL, 82
HOLMES, 30 35 39 43 46 47 49 52
56 59 66 74 76 77 84 88 93 94
96 97 99 104 105

HOLT, 62 90 92 101 104
HOPKINS, 1 7 26 30 34 60 63 65
66
HORSINGTON, 55
HORSLEY, 68
HOSKINS, 5 10 12 16 36 38
HOUGH, 11
HOWARD, 63
HUCHANS, 102
HUDDLESTONE, 84 86
HUGGINS, 101 104
HUGINS, 32 80
HUMPHREY, 13 36
HUNT, 8
HUNTER, 6 10 17 25 30 35 38 43
46 54 64 66 70 75 78-81 83 87
88 89 92 95 97 98-100 103-105
HUSON, 26
HUTCHASON, 34
HUTCHINGS, 38 39 55 57 71 91
HUTCHINSON, 34 40 43 44 51 52
53
IDLE, 74
ILIFFE, 27
ILISSE, 1
INCE, 84 95 98 103
ISDELL, 50
IVES, 35 69
IVEY, 1
IVY, 2 3 6 11 13 16 18 21 32 39 47
50 51 57 59 61 72 75 78 84 93
JACKSON, 1 3 7 24 33 60 80
JACOB, 88 89 93 96 98
JAMASON, 33
JAMES, 4 18 24 29 34 46 47 53 57
59 60 66 70 73 79 95 98 100
101
JAMESON, 70 73 78 83 84 86 88
94 98
JAMIESON, 98
JAMISON, 30 31 102
JARVES, 22 34
JARVIS, 54
JEAMASON, 64
JENKINS, 27
JOHNSON, 17 18 21 23 27 29 35
37 68 72 87
JOLLEY, 60
JONES, 1 5
6 8 12 15 16 17 18 20
21 22 27 29-31 35-38

JONES (continued)
43-51 53 55 56 62 67-70 73 80
82-84 88 89 93 105
JOUSLIN, 11
KAVENING, 1
KAY, 102
KEATON, 12 18 36 37 38 50 96
KEEL, 63
KEELING, 1 3-7 10 13 20 22 25
34 35 38 39 42 44 45 51 56 57
59 65 67 69 73 74 76-81 83-86
90-94 96 97 99-105
KELLEE, 1
KELLEY, 42 59 93
KEMP, 5 11 23-26 29 35 41 72
KEMPE, 1 3 8 37 47 48 51 52 56
59 61 63 65 67 68 70 71 74 75
78-84 87 89 92 96 101-105
KENSEY, 6 17 42
KENTON, 27
KESER, 76
KEY, 73 89 90
KILLEY, 17 65
KING, 98
KINGMAN, 41 43 44 47 49
KINGSTONE, 23
KINSE, 6
KNOWIS, 63 66 70 99
LABRITTOONE, 2
LAMAN, 16
LAMBART, 49
LAMOND, 62
LAMOUNT, 3-5 7 9 12 14 25-27
30-32 39 52 58 59 61 67 68 84
86 89 93 98 99 102 105
LAND, 2 7-9 23 24 27 29 30 32
36 46 47 49-53 56 58 65 69 71
73 75 78 84 89 91 96 99 100
103-105
LANE, 15 17 28 68 89
LANGLEY, 29 41 46 70 72 81 85
89 93 102
LATIMER, 102
LATTER, 57 60 88
LAWLEY, 55
LAWN, 16
LAWSON, 2 3 4 8 10 12 14 16
19-22 24 32 49 62 70 80 89 90-
92 94 97-99 102 103
LEAMOUNT, 39 44 51

LEARY, 19
LEE, 1 10
LEETIH, 101
LEFESLEY, 45
LEGAT, 34
LEGATT, 72
LEGGET, 37 42 45 50 93 94
LEGGETT, 15 47
LEGREW, 74
LENARD, 35 74
LESTER, 4 5 6 26 30 61 62 75 78
85 87 88 98 105
LEVINGSTONE, 6
LEWELLING, 80
LEWIS, 4 10 11 18 21 27
LILBURN, 30 35 38 43 44 50 52
60 68 72 76 79
LINAHAN, 83
LINSEY, 18
LINTON, 25 29 42 53
LOCKHART, 76
LOOSLEY, 38
LOOSLY, 49
LOVE, 14 72 74
LOVET, 35 39 44 46
LOVETT, 1 3-6 7 10 20 34 38 42
44 54 64 66 67 75 78 81 83 84
90-93 97 99 100 103-105
LOVIT, 35
LOVITT, 25 28
LOWERY, 39
LOWRY, 29 31
LURREY, 19
LURRY, 21 46
LYBURN, 8
LYBURNE, 16
MACARTY, 14
MACASSLON, 78
MACKCLALIN, 61
MACKEEL, 62
MACKIE, 7 13 14 17 21 25 26 30
39 41 44 86
MACKLAN, 44
MACLANAHAN, 12
MACLOUD, 21 30 48 62
MACOY, 22 26
MAGRAVY, 11 38
MAJOR, 96
MAKEEL, 15
MALALAHAN, 28

Other Heritage Books by Anne E. Maling:

CD: Guardian Accounts of Princess Anne County, Virginia, 1736–1871

CD: Princess Anne County, Virginia Land and Probate Records, 1691–1783
Volumes 1–18 Abstracted from Deed Books

CD: Princess Anne County, Virginia Wills, 1783–1871

CD: Princess Anne County, Virginia Deeds, Wills, and Guardianships

Guardian Accounts of Princess Anne County, Virginia

Princess Anne County, Virginia Land and Probate Records
Abstracted from Deed Books One to Eighteen, 1691–1783

Princess Anne County, Virginia Land and Probate Records
Abstracted from Deed Books One to Seven, 1691–1755

Princess Anne County, Virginia Land and Probate Records
Abstracted from Deed Books Eight to Eighteen, 1691–1783

Princess Anne County, Virginia Wills, 1783–1871

www.ingramcontent.com/pod-product-compliance
Lightning Source LLC
Chambersburg PA
CBHW071835090426
42737CB00012B/2251